Side Hustle & Flow

Side Hustle & Flow

Cliff Beach

THE **BLACK SPRING**
PRESS GROUP

First published in 2023
An Eyewear Publishing book, The Black Spring Press Group
Grantully Road, Maida Vale, London W9
United Kingdom

Cover Art ImageStricken

The author has requested the publisher use American spelling and grammar wherever possible in this edition

ISBN-13 978-1-915406-41-5

FSC www.fsc.org MIX Paper from responsible sources FSC® C018072

I dedicate this book to my loving mom, Tonya, who sacrificed everything to bring me into this world, and who never stops supporting me, telling me how much she loves me, and saying how much I make her proud to be my mom.

Contents

Acknowledgements

I would like to thank and acknowledge:

- Todd & Black Spring Press Group for all their work in getting the book published
- Brian Tracy for his endorsement testimonial and wonderful book writing course
- Tucker Max and Scribe Media for their amazing, free writing and publishing courses
- Chandler Bolt & Self Publishing school for his free writing and publishing resources
- Tim Ferris for sparking the dream to make a podcast and a book
- Blake Bauer for also sparking the dream to make a book
- Mookie and 885FM for helping me build a platform
- James & Beautytap for employing me while creating this book
- Deborah Sosin for Editing
- Jenna Love-Shrader for Editing and Proofreading
- Jill for always being encouraging
- Bryan Cohen & Selling for Authors for your 5 Day Amazon Ads Challenge
- Tony Robbins & Dean Graziosi for your Comeback Challenges
- Ricardo Fayet & Reedsy for a great writer's tool and marketplace
- Kindra Hall & Success Magazine/Success Achievers Community for her Book Live Masterclass

Introduction

> *"I think it's really important to feed the side hustle. Do what you have to do to make ends meet, but aim to diversify, dream and feed the hustle because you never know where it might take you."*
> –Sunny Hostin, Emmy winning co-host of ABC's *The View*

I once attended a support group for people seeking work and met a man who said that when he wasn't working, he felt great joy in salsa dancing. I asked him, "If you know exactly what you love to do, why aren't you doing that as much as possible?"

This is the question at the heart of this book. If you know what you could be doing to feel happier and more fulfilled, and you are not doing it now, why not? If you don't know the answer right now, that's okay.

Believe me, I feel your pain. Sometimes it takes feeling lost in order to begin the journey of finding yourself again. I was once lost just like you. You either do not know your purpose or you are not fully walking in your purpose today, and that's tough. For many of you, life just happened, things came up unexpectedly, and you did the best you could but didn't quite hit the mark.

I am here to show you how I was able to find the balance between achieving fulfillment and doing the work that I love while still working a day job and living well.

In This Book, You Will Learn:

- How you can have the life you want now
- How everyone has a purpose, and you can find yours
- How to run your life like a booming business
- How to start now or start going faster/harder
- How to stop surviving and start thriving

- How to delegate
- How to build your dream on the side while working a day job
- How to have work/life balance
- How successful people live

Two things that are especially important:

- The day you were born is not as good as the day you find out why you were born. You have a purpose.
- Many people are living passionless lives and feel devoid of purpose. Let's rekindle that passionate fire inside of you.

My Background

I am an international award-winning musician, songwriter, TEDX speaker, Toastmaster, and entrepreneur. I have an MBA from Pepperdine University and a BM in Music Business Management from Berklee College of Music. I am a Distinguished Toastmaster and member of Toastmasters International based in Culver City, California. Credentials aside, I have found a way to afford the lifestyle I desire while doing the passion projects that I love—that is, working a day gig and maintaining several side hustles. I have created my own path of enlightenment, fulfillment, and success, and I would like to share my journey and experiences with you in the hopes of helping you do the same.

What This Book Is And Isn't

This book is for fans of self-help books who are feeling stuck in the rat race and want to have more passionate, purpose-filled lives. It is *not* for anyone looking for a quick fix. As bestselling author Dave Ramsey says, "Opportunity shows up often wearing work clothes." It will not be easy, and it will require a lot of grit and self-discipline, but I am confident that by the end of this book, you will have the advanced tools you need to start living a better, more fulfilled life.

Are you ready to start REALLY living? If so, keep reading.

1.

Why Not You, Why Not Now?

> *"Today, many will decide to no longer sit back with a victim mentality, but to take charge of their lives and make positive changes. Why not you?"* —Steve Maraboli, author of Life, the Truth, and Being Free

In the winter of 2003, I moved to the City of Angels from Beantown to pursue music, with nothing but the clothes on my back, a song, and a dream. That year, I got kicked off the highly popular reality TV show *American Idol*, and from those ashes, I started my first band.

I had just graduated from Berklee College of Music and celebrated my twentieth birthday. Here I was, embarking on a scary, exciting new journey of leaving behind everything I knew and trying to make it in one of the most difficult cities in the entertainment industry. If I had known just how difficult it would be, or if I had waited, I most likely would have chickened out.

I arrived with a friend from school who, luckily, knew someone who was renting an apartment in what is affectionately known as "Culver City Adjacent" (near the "Black Target Store") on La Cienega Boulevard. I spent my first weeks in L.A. living the starving artist dream—which meant eating ramen noodles. I soon lost forty pounds and spent my days scouring the internet looking for my first of many dead-end office jobs.

Holy Grail

At that time, one of the best ways to "make it" was to audition for the wildly popular show *American Idol*. I slept outside of the Rose Bowl in

Pasadena for three days in the elements, all for a chance to be humiliated on TV. While waiting in line, I randomly ran into an old friend from Berklee. We huddled together for warmth as we eagerly awaited our turn to get wristbands and sing in front of the judges. What they don't show you on TV is that it's a huge cattle call audition, and they eliminate most who audition before they ever get on TV.

I made it through the first round, which was outside at the bowl, in the sweltering sun, surrounded by thousands of people. It was a challenge for all of us to have tight vocals, but I think they wanted to subject us to the pressure of performing under high-intensity stress. The producers lined us up in groups of ten and went down the row, asking us to sing for thirty seconds, either giving us callbacks or eliminating us on the spot. I won a spot belting out the apropos "Living for the City," originally performed by my idol, Stevie Wonder. I was told to move forward into a line where I then received information on the next callback on a piece of paper. From there, the staff said that I would need to go to Hollywood in the next few weeks for my next audition. I thought this was going to be my big ticket outta the drudgery of job hunting and the prospect of office life. During the next round, I got to meet Simon Fuller, the executive producer, who said that he "loved me" (don't they all?) and passed me to the next round.

I was anticipating finally being on TV and meeting Randy Jackson, Paula Abdul, and Simon Cowell. Only I didn't actually meet Paula. They said she was sick and didn't show, so instead I was judged by Randy, Simon, and Ryan Seacrest, who filled in for Paula. I was booted after that round, and the only thing that remains of my Idol experience is a clip showing me getting sent home, shrugging, and saying that I didn't get my "golden ticket" to Hollywood.

Afterward, I went to eat at California Pizza Kitchen with my parents, who had driven up from Riverside. I numbly sat there, eating crappy pizza, feeling sick to my stomach, and thinking my life was over. I did not know it at the time, but ironically my career was just beginning.

> *There is no reason you can't do and have what you want—unless, you believe you can't or aren't actually pursuing your desires.*

It Starts With Belief In Yourself

Your entire life can change in the blink of an eye. Storms can come in and rock you to the core. When *American Idol* ended for me, I retreated for a bit to lick my wounds. I left feeling not only disappointed but extremely angry. *How dare they piss all over my dream?* I thought. I started to doubt myself, but I eventually learned two unbelievably valuable lessons at that moment:

1. Never doubt yourself.
2. Never stop pursuing your dreams.

Setbacks are temporary and a natural occurrence on the road to success. So I figured I better get used to them. That's part of my lesson for you too. Simon, Randy, and Ryan Seacrest did me a huge favor by releasing me from the dream of finding musical stardom on TV. My real dream was to be a *musician*, not to win *American Idol*. I had to shift my mindset. Ultimately, I knew that I had everything inside me to accomplish this dream. I went back home, chatted with my drummer roommate, and declared that no matter what, we were going to get our band together—*now!* I used that disappointment and anger as a catalyst to start my first band, The Moon Crickets.

But how did I find the strength to continue to muck uphill and make my dream a reality? Luckily, I am a naturally motivated and driven person. I'm also very self-reliant and resilient.

To believe in yourself is to "feel sure of truth." What is your truth? I had always heard the phrase tossed around, "Stand in your truth." That is how you learn to believe in yourself. *Belief is faith*. Sometimes you must believe in something that is unseen. *Belief is hope.*

I had to start believing that I could do anything I set my mind to and hope that it was going to work out if I tried hard enough and was persistent. Was it easy? Hell no! Nothing ever is. Theodore Roosevelt said, *"Nothing in the world is worth having or worth doing unless it means effort, pain, difficulty."*[1] Belief in yourself can certainly be difficult and painful,

1 Reel 421, Theodore Roosevelt, "Theodore Roosevelt papers," Manuscript Division, Library of Congress, Washington D.C.

and the process is not effortless. You will constantly battle fear, doubt, negative feedback, and hundreds of other forces. Like gravity, these forces have the ability to continually pull you down. It takes effort to get out of bed, get dressed, and battle all day on your nine-to-five, then be the weekend warrior for your dream.

The type of belief in myself I had to have was met with a childlike naivety. At age twenty, I was too dumb to know that I had a snowball's chance in hell of succeeding, but I believed in myself enough to try. I knew that if I didn't act, there was a 100 percent chance I wouldn't find success.

Positive Thinking

I want to make it clear that believing in yourself is not a catch-all to suddenly make you invincible or a superhero. No matter how much I believe in myself, I cannot do things that I am not equipped for. For example, if you were in a car accident and were rushed into surgery, I could not suddenly become a surgeon and begin operating on you. I am not a doctor; therefore you would surely die. When delving into self-help books (and I have read a ton) I think it is easy for the theories of *belief in yourself* and *positive thinking* to be misconstrued.

I wake up every morning believing it is going to be a good day. Does that mean it never rains and that I never have problems? No! That would be theoretically impossible. But now I approach each day in the same way, with the same mantras I have said and read to myself for years:

> *I believe in myself.*
>
> *I believe I can have good things in life and that good things will happen for me.*
>
> *I believe I must work hard and put in the effort in order to receive abundance.*

Positive thinking sometimes makes people think they can be unrealistic. I am a realist. I live in the real world. But thinking positively has many benefits that I never found when I was thinking negatively. Positivity is a magnet pulling you upward, making you feel lighter; negativity is a magnet pulling you downward, making you feel heavier.

What Do You Believe?

What are you telling yourself? Whether you believe you can or you can't, you're right. The mind is immensely powerful, and having the right mindset is the key to getting where you want to be. One of the most powerful exercises I learned from Lisa Nichols' book, *No Matter What*, is to press Pause on the tape deck in my head to interrupt the negative feedback loop, and press Play on the positive feedback loop.

That one statement changed my life. Over the years, throughout my struggles and search for success, I battled with drinking and suffered the artist's depressive mindset. I felt bombarded by so many negative thoughts that I could not think straight. When I was twenty-five years old, I started having panic attacks and was diagnosed with an anxiety disorder and prescribed Ativan and Valium for my condition. I do not like taking pills; I actually have difficulty swallowing them. So, after a few weeks, I decided not to take them and chose to heal myself with herbal teas and meditation instead, while also cutting out stimulants and changing my own personal narrative—what I believed.

Was it easy? No. I still suffered for about two years before I got a handle on it, but now I have no more heart palpitations, no shortness of breath, no dizzy spells—all because I believed I could get better and changed my mindset about myself and my life.

I know that some of you reading this are thinking, *It is not that easy for me, Cliff. You got lucky*. Maybe you are right. I do feel lucky that I was able to overcome my situation without medication. I am sensitive to that and medicine can be exceptionally good for many people, as can therapy.

However for me, I discovered that my anxiety was rooted in negative beliefs about myself. When I started believing differently and making positive changes, the needle moved. Note that the natural, nonmedical approach takes more time and is not a quick fix.

What Do You Really Want?

Motivational speaker and author Zig Ziglar said, "*You can get what you want if you help enough others get what they want.*" For others to get what they want, or for you to ultimately get what you want, you have to define and refine what it is that you want most out of life or out of the projects and goals you have set for yourself. Many people have never taken the time to ask themselves what they want because they are afraid or ignorant of the fact that to get to an answer, you have to first ask questions.

Some people are conditioned by experiences and their upbringing to not want very much. My dad would always say to me, "I keep my wants very low." I always thought that was a terrible way to live. I always wanted more for myself, and I know both of my parents wanted more for me than they had, but my dad did not want it enough for himself.

I heard it described by preacher Eric Thomas in this way: *"When you want to succeed as badly as you want to breathe, then you will be successful."* You cannot just simply want it, you must *really* want it, as the work it takes to get what you want is a long, arduous task. Whether you want to lose weight, run a marathon, get a promotion, start a business, or start a family, you have to know what you want and then pursue it with the reckless abandon it will take to be successful.

But again, it all comes back to knowing what you want. To want is "to have a desire or wish to possess or do something." What do you want to have, and what do you want to do? After my *American Idol* debacle, I wanted to start my own band (what I wanted to do), and I wanted to have my own album (what I wanted to have).

The Moon Crickets was quickly formed by adding in a bass player, whom we met from Craigslist, and a guitar player, whom I had met singing backgrounds in another friend's band, Homestyle. We rehearsed and started playing shows for at least two years before we were able to finally record and release our debut album, *The Moon Crickets LP,* in 2006 (which was financed by our old landlord, who had made some extra money from the sale of our first apartment).

So, three years after *American Idol*, I got some of what I wanted. I had the band and the album, but was that everything I wanted? No. Our wants and needs change and evolve over time. Ten years from now I may want something completely different, and that is okay. I was content at the time but constantly looking for ways to continue to improve.

Wanting Things That Are BAD For You

If the thing you want badly is bad for you, then it will have a negative result. I am not advocating something that leads toward a substance addiction or infringes on someone else's happiness or civil liberties. Even too much of a good thing can be a bad thing. If you drink too much carrot juice, your skin will turn orange from the beta carotene overload; if you work out too much, you will injure yourself; if you drink too much, you will get sick or possibly die. You must continue to live in balance and moderation.

Wanting GOOD Things

Proverbs 18:22 says, *"He who finds a wife finds a good thing."* There are two main points I pull from this scripture: you have to seek to find something, and finding what you are looking for can be a good thing. Wanting to lose weight and get healthy, wanting to learn a new piece of music, or wanting to find a mate are all good things. So when you find/do them, you should feel good about yourself and the result.

Let's deconstruct the "what" of what I wanted. I wanted to move to L.A. *Check.* I wanted to find and go on auditions. *Check* and *check.* I wanted to start a band, write, perform, produce, record my own music, and release it. *Check. Check. Check. Check. Check* and *Check.* And that is just a short list of what I wanted. (I also wanted to make money, get a girlfriend, travel, be a good son, and many other things, but for now we narrow the scope.) All of these on their own are good things, but there is one important fact we will touch on next.

You Can Have Everything, But Not All At Once

Would you eat a five-course meal all at once? I hope not! Because you would likely not be fully tasting and enjoying the meal in the way the chef intended. You could even make yourself sick. There are many natural laws at work that you cannot circumvent. No matter how hard I try, I cannot walk through walls, and you cannot have everything you want all at once either, and for good reason.

When I was a young thespian in community summer dinner theatre in college, I always wanted a lead part but would be relegated to the chorus. Roberta, my director at the time, would continually tell me, *"You get the part that you are ready for at that time."* I was not lead material at that time. I had not gone through adequate preparation, and the roles I was going for were not tailor-made for me. Now I wish she could see all the music videos I have made, in which I'm the lead in my own stories, tailor-made to me. But I realize if I had not toiled in the background, I would never have built the chops and self-awareness to create my own thing. Don't spend time trying to fit into a mold that is not for you when you need to break away and make your own.

Why Are You Holding Yourself Back?

If you tether an animal to a post with a rope or chain, you will inevitably restrict its movement. This can be literal or metaphorical. Michael Singer, author of *The Untethered Soul,* stated:

> *"Truth is only complicated because we pass it through our habitual thought patterns. When we step back from ourselves, truth becomes simple. There are not many paths to freedom, there is only one."*[2]

Let's unpack this for a moment. We overcomplicate our truth. You must first admit you have been holding yourself back. Holding yourself back with excuses for all your past failures. Holding yourself back from past hurt and regrets. We tend to overcomplicate the simple. How do we even know what our truth is if we pass it through habitual thought patterns that are not serving us well? Have we challenged our preconceived notions and assumptions to know if they are true or valid?

Let's say you want to be a chef. If you were constantly told, "*You are not good enough,*" you may believe that as your truth. You may think everything you make is garbage. You are not going to become an award-winning chef with that attitude, and on some level, you might even know it is not true. You are good enough, and most likely most of what you make

2 Michael Singer, "The Untethered Soul: The Journey Beyond Yourself" https://www.huffpost.com/entry/spiritual-awakening-super-soul-sunday_b_1729 741.

is good, sometimes even great. Sometimes we are too close to a situation to see it objectively. We must take a step back to gain perspective. Then the truth becomes clearer and simpler. There is one option to set yourself free—to sever the tether to the negative voices.

Like Hebrews 12:1 says, we must *"throw off everything that hinders us."* If you are tethered, you will not be able to move onward and upward. So many people in life are tethered to old information, old relationships, and old ideals that are no longer beneficial. For some, it is easy to let go; but for others, it is not. Forgiveness is one of the hardest things you can learn to do. Sometimes you must forgive someone who is no longer around. And the hardest person to forgive is yourself. But in the end, only in freedom can we walk in the true path toward our goals, dreams, and aspirations. You cannot climb the mountain tethered to a boulder at the base. That would be a death sentence.

The Fear Monster

I know I have held myself back in my life because of fear. I was afraid my music might not be good enough. I'd think, *What if no one listens? What if it gets bad reviews?* The list goes on and on. Susan Jeffers, in her landmark book *Feel the Fear and Do It Anyway*, remarks:

> *"Often we think, 'I'll do it when I am not afraid. But in reality, it works the other way around. The "doing it" comes before the fear goes away. The only way to get rid of the fear of doing something is to go out and do it.'"*[3]

My fear started to dissipate as I started to work on my craft. Each album, song, and single got easier; therefore, I became less fearful because I had more under my belt. But the first ones were difficult. The good thing is when I started, I was writing alone, so no one heard the songs that weren't good. It is a process and progression. I realized it is okay if my music isn't good. It is okay if no one listens to it. It is okay if my album

3 Susan Jeffers, "Eight 'Feel the Fear' Tips for Building Confidence and Peace of Mind" http://www.visionworx.co.za/2011/03/feel-the-fear-and-doit-anyway-susan-jeffers/.

gets bad reviews or no reviews at all. The bar was low. In my own way of thinking, success was starting the project and seeing it to the finish line. Changing my expectations combined with the sheer power of doing it made the fear monster become smaller and smaller over time. Leaving fear in the past, I found I was no longer tethered to it. When I reflect back on my past now, fear was like a mountain: close up, it was large and looming, but in the distance the fear became smaller under a new perspective, and while I was moving toward my goal and away from the fear.

The Failure Monster

No one likes to fail. I lost out in the Lennon Awards recently, and that stung. But wrapped in every failure there is a teachable moment, a lesson to be learned. I have heard the terms "failing forward" or "failing upward," and they both ring true. The Moon Crickets was as much a success as it was a failure. I toiled hard with that band from 2003 to 2007, and then, after two albums, we disbanded. In those four years, it was exceedingly difficult but also extremely rewarding. I could have seen it as a failure. The band, eventually, didn't share my same vision, and we never got that record deal. But it was not a failure. If anything, it was just one chapter ending and a new one beginning. Plus, I left that group with the experience of two albums under my belt (one in the studio and one live), working with an investor, producers, and engineers. I also learned both what to do and not to do next time. Experience is invaluable; failure is its best teacher.

Almost anyone who was/is successful has failed, so you are in good company. The father of the automotive industry, Henry Ford, is remembered as saying, *"Failure is simply the opportunity to begin again, this time more intelligently."*[4] From JK Rowling to Steve Jobs to Michael Jordan to Albert Einstein, all failed on their path to success. Rowling was on welfare; Jobs was forced out of Apple; Jordan missed thousands of shots; and Einstein failed his school entrance exam. Einstein, a Nobel

4 Henry Ford, "Daily Quote: Failure is Simply the Opportunity to Begin Again" https://www.lifehack.org/articles/productivity/daily-quote-failure-simply-the-opportunity-begin-again.html.

Prize winner, believed that *"success is failure in progress."* Anyone who has succeeded has failed bigger and often more publicly than you.

The Fame Monster

Once you overcome the other fears and failure, you must also be wary of the fame monster. In the journey to become more fulfilled and live with purpose, you may think, *Oh God, what if I do become famous, what then?* With fame comes access and opportunity but also criticism and scrutiny. You may not want to be in the public eye. One of the greatest examples of this is one of my heroes, Michael Jackson.

I idolized MJ growing up, wanting to be like Mike. I admired his talent and vision as it pertained to his work ethic, longevity, legacy, and sheer artistic prowess. But he was not the poster child for happiness. Fame robbed him of any type of normalcy; he had tons of psychological issues, and he died ravaged by the media, a prisoner in his own house, addicted to overprescribed drugs. His scandals, his controversies, his plastic surgeries—it was all on display on a world stage for all to dissect. He was a great businessman, but it cost him friendships. He did not know who to trust. Being famous comes at a price.

In many ways MJ and other famous people live in what I call the Willy Wonka Fantasy Fallacy. At the end of the movie in *Willy Wonka and the Chocolate Factory*, Charlie has won the golden ticket and survived all the hazards of the Oompa-Loompas. One single act of kindness gets Charlie everything he wanted, and he lives happily ever after. But getting everything you wanted can often not be what it is all cracked up to be. Life is not a fairytale or a movie, and fame can often become a person's undoing. Fame is the byproduct of success, never the end goal. People used to be famous for something they *did*, but social media and reality TV have made people famous for doing nothing. Either way, fame is something you must keep in check lest you self-destruct from it.

Make Your Own Way

When my band imploded, just like when *American Idol* blew up in my face, I had a mourning period. There was a temporary moment when I felt my life was over, and in a way it was. Whenever we experience a great loss or disappointment, it is like experiencing a death. The old me was dead. The me before that situation was gone, and the new me was reborn, instantly. Sure, I could wallow in self-pity for a while, but eventually I either had to get up and move on or fall deeper into despair. The great motivational speaker and storyteller Les Brown tells the story of a gentleman walking down the street who comes across a house with a man and a dog sitting on the front porch. The dog is moaning and groaning loudly, so the gentleman calls out to the man on the porch and asks, "What's wrong with your dog?"

The man replies to the gentleman, "He's lying on a nail."

The gentleman, in shock, asks the man, "Why doesn't the dog move?"

The man retorts, "It hurts him enough to complain but not enough to do something about it."

Who has ever found themselves in that situation?

Complaining In Complacency

When trying to make your own way, it is easier to complain and do nothing than to get up and do something about it. Often, new inventions and ideas are brought about through great pain. John Walsh is the creator of *America's Most Wanted*, a remarkably successful anti-crime television program that ran for several seasons. The show was created in the aftermath of the abduction and murder of his son, Adam. It would have been easy for Walsh to wallow in the wake of his own tragedy, but instead he turned his situation into a vehicle to help bring many criminals to justice and provide families with closure. Complaining, which was very much his right, would not have yielded much. It would not bring his son back; it would just add to the large vacuum of white noise in a complex and chaotic world.

Many artists I run in to are waiting for *someone else* to come along before they get their art out there. They are waiting for a manager, agent, music supervisor, producer, or someone else to help push their work. With the dawn of the digital age and the democratization of technology, tools and resources are rapidly and readily more available to everyone. The days of waiting around for a record deal are over, which is not such a bad thing because most record deals are terrible for the artist, and many times the work never sees the light of day. Now, you can easily get your music or your art to the masses through the internet 100 percent on your own.

After the dust settled from The Moon Crickets being no more, I emerged to start playing new music under my own name, Cliff Beach, for the first time in my life. I was not just the front man; I was the band leader and the face of my brand. I started making music again in 2010 after a brief hiatus to attend business school (see the MBA after my name) and released my first EP, the award-nominated *Who the Funk Is Cliff Beach?* in 2013. No money or investors this time, just me in a friend's home studio figuring out how to produce on my own.

That album was not meant to catapult me into stardom but rather to be a proof of concept. It was to prove to myself that I could do it on my own, not in the shadow of a band, but as a solo artist. Hindsight is twenty-twenty. If I knew then what I know now, I would have done so many things differently and made an even better record, but that is the beauty of learning during the journey and using that knowledge in your next project.

Necessity Is The Mother Of Invention

When I set out to make my own music many years ago, I just wanted to sing. I did not set out to originally become a keyboard player, arranger, songwriter, lyricist, producer, publisher, and record label owner, but that is exactly what happened. I did not know I would become a top liner, teach at writing camps overseas, and license music in Hong Kong, Japan, and Korea. All I wanted to do was sing. And I still do!

In my desire to grow, become better, and make myself more marketable, it just organically happened that I would become all the other things. I never dreamed that my label would eventually go on to release records by other groups and that we would become an authority in the space and give master classes on the subject of creating vinyl in the digital age. I'm just a singer.

But I am not just a singer. I am a singer with an MBA. We are a rare breed. I am equally as creative as I am analytical and, working for small businesses, I am used to wearing many hats. (I am also bald, so literally

I am always wearing a hat.) No one is just one thing. Even Shaq rapped and acted (five Billboard Hot 100 hits, nineteen film credits, not to mention the long-forgotten video game *Shaq Fu*). I am not going to debate the merit of those other ventures; we all know he was a much better NBA player (15-time NBA All-Star, four-time NBA Champion, and Olympic gold medalist). The point is, he was able to do other things he had not originally set out to do. When learning to make it on your own, you are going to adapt and pick up new skills you didn't know you had, or could learn, to make your dream a reality.

You're Your Own Boss

Poet William Ernest, in *Invictus* (which means "unconquered" in Latin), penned these immortal words: *"I am the master of my fate: I am the captain of my soul,"*[5] to which author Michael Josephson concluded, "*You are the captain of your own ship; don't let anyone take the wheel.*"[6] I work for a small cosmetics company as the head of digital. We often find ourselves saying, "*You have to drive that bus,*" meaning you have to wholly own that project you are working on.

Your life is that bus, and it is up to you as the driver to keep it on the road and steer it where you want to go. You have your GPS inside you, and you have the visibility to see hazards ahead and swerve around them. Sometimes there will be accidents, but you will get patched up and get back on the road.

Unfortunately, there is no Uber bus, and no driverless bus; no one can drive that bus but you. No one else has the key and can start it, and only you have access to the GPS that is hardwired into your spirit, soul, mind, and DNA.

But sometimes being your own boss sucks. Who do you complain to about your boss—yourself? It is like owning a house. You are your own

5 William Ernest Henley, "Invictus" https://www.invictus.education/invictus-poem/.

6 Quote by Michael Josephson: "You are the captain of your [...]" https://www.goodreads.com/quotes/507637-you-are-the-captain-of-your-own-ship-don-t-let.

landlord, and when something breaks, it is up to you and you alone to fix it. Murphy's Law is in full effect, and anything that can go wrong, will. But just like owning a home, the equity goes up in value over time. The sweat equity of being your own boss also rises in value over time. Investing in yourself is always a great choice.

Even if you are currently working for someone else (I work for a company as aforementioned), you are still your own boss. Why? Your job is basically a micro version of the entire company. You have an employee (you) and stakeholders (everyone else). You have clients (coworkers and customers), and you must deal with finance (money), politics, meetings, IT (computers), and other functions. Your input matters and should be adding to the value of your firm—or why else do it? The days of merely being an employee are over. Companies don't want that arrangement and cannot afford it. They don't need more Dilberts and worker bees; they need people who can creatively and critically think for themselves. Be a boss! Period.

How Can You Improve?

I am an earnest believer that you can continually improve, from your first breath until the day you die. As a working musician for over twenty years, I can attest that practice and experimentation is a lifelong learned skill. Even the best virtuosos, from Chick Corea to Yo-Yo Ma to Béla Fleck, constantly practice. I recall hearing motivational speaker Zig Ziglar say that he would still practice and improve a speech he had given hundreds of times because he never wanted to get sloppy or become so overconfident that he could forgo practice and just wing it.

Do you focus on your weaknesses or play to your strengths? It sounds nice to build up things that you are not good at, but it is time consuming. If you are at a point in your life when you want to move forward and maximize your talents, I believe you need to play to your strengths first and foremost. You must take a self-inventory of what you are good at. When I started studying music in conservatory at age sixteen, I had already spent my entire childhood in piano lessons, gospel choir, chamber singers, and both high school and all-state chorus, and I was starting at the bottom with kids who already had a list of credits under their belt.

When I got to Berklee, all I did was practice, go to class, and learn as much as I could in the library.

A lot of kids at Berklee peaked too early, resting on their laurels and never improving. I, on the other hand, was the underdog, the Rocky Balboa of the group. I had to work to improve. I recall trying out for the Singer's Showcase, the most coveted show in our school, which showcased the best of the best in front of a packed audience of critical-eared, musician peers. I was rejected six times in a row, only to get in as a duet with my best friend (who had done it previously) on lucky number seven. I remember the sixth time getting rejected. My duet partner and I tried to go eat after the auditions, and I had that same sick feeling I had in my stomach after the *American Idol* rejection, but I again came to the same realization: I would persist. I spent that entire semester working on my craft, putting on more shows, directing shows, choreographing musicals, taking all the feedback given to me and trying new things to get better and improve. When we went into the seventh audition, we made sure that we were so prepared, so solid that they would have no choice but to let us in, and they did. And then once we got in, we didn't stop there. We were super selective about our song choices. We had extra rehearsals with the background vocalists, and we agonized over our outfits. We wanted everything to be perfect.

Finally, on the night of the show, we were the only duo, and we were set to perform in the opening and closing ensemble numbers, as well as the closing act of each of the two sets. What I remember most is seeing the faces in the audience and hearing their voices cheering loudly for our renditions of Aretha Franklin, Tammi Terrell, Marvin Gaye, and James Brown covers. But how did "just another kid from somewhere" leave his small-pond suburb in Maryland, near D.C., to go to Boston and make a splash in a big music pond like Berklee (one of the top contemporary music conservatories in the world)? How did he go from obscure to very well known in the best performance at the biggest showcase of the school year? By living the motto:

ALWAYS BE IMPROVING!

The Karate Kid

The movie *The Karate Kid* is a good example of how we can improve ourselves. Mr. Miyagi gives Daniel San so many menial tasks, such as painting fences and waxing the car, that seemingly have nothing to do with learning the ancient martial arts. Who wants to spend all their time doing chores? I am sure Daniel San thought Mr. Miyagi was just sweating him for free slave labor, but the old man was also incredibly wise. We as the audience get to go on this journey through the movie and see it finally all click that the motions learned in painting fences and waxing the car aren't meaningless, menial tasks; they are actually the foundation and building blocks for Daniel San to learn karate.

I have been a music teacher and mentor for many years, and I teach all students basically the same thing; we start with the fundamentals. Learning the notes and scales are tried-and-true skills. In the same way you would not build a house without a foundation, there is no way to understand music on an academic level without understanding notes and scales. They are the building blocks for harmony, chords, and anything else in the music theory arsenal.

This process is a metaphor for life. Whether you work in the arts or fly a plane for a living, when it comes to self-improvement, it is always built on a solid foundation. What do you want to learn? What are your core strengths? How can you improve on the processes, and what you are already doing?

James P. Lewis, in *Working Together*, writes *"If you always do what you've always done, you'll always get what you always get."* It is universally accepted that the definition of insanity is doing the exact same thing and expecting a different result. I took a Masterclass online from jazz master Herbie Hancock, and his approach to practice and improving stemmed from his Buddhist roots.

You could tell he was not just purely focused on becoming a better musician but a better person. It was not just about doing; it was about being. Making that connection is particularly important to evolving and improving. Sometimes you are going to receive feedback that you do not understand, or you must work with little information and figure out how you can use this to improve your approach and way of thinking.

Herbie tells a story about Miles Davis, who was esoteric and often hard to understand. Perhaps because he did a lot of drugs and because he had a gravelly voice due to having had a botched throat surgery. Miles turns to Herbie during a gig and tells him, "Herbie, I said don't play those butter notes. No more butter notes." In real time, Herbie is thinking to himself, *What is this MF talking about? What in the hell is a butter note?* Herbie later starts thinking more about this and decides that it means to trim the fat, scrape off the cream, play more simply, and leave some notes out of the thickly voiced jazz chords he had been playing. He says that it was a pivotal moment in his music career, and it totally changed his future approach to playing music. And we will never know if this was what Miles meant, or perhaps it was just a crazy coked-up jazz head spouting out what only made sense to him. Nevertheless, Herbie decided to take the critique and ceased to play "butter notes."

When You Were Little, What Did You Want To Be?

I have watched the TED Talks of the late Sir Ken Robinson on creativity and education reform, which I highly recommend. His information echoes what I know about the devastation caused by the government defunding art and music programs in schools. He basically says that you can ask a room of kindergarteners if they consider themselves creative, and almost everyone will raise their hands. But ask the same question when those kids get to the end of high school, and almost no one raises their hands. He theorizes that school robs children of creativity, making them fearful to stick out, forcing them to fit into one way of learning and thinking.

Many children are left behind because they may have different learning styles (like learning by doing) or may not be able to excel at learning from books. When you talk to kids about what they want to do when they grow up, you will hear them shout out, "I want to be a ballerina!" "I am going to be a policeman!" "I want to be a doctor." You never hear a child say, "I want to work a mediocre job in middle management." This scenario reminds me of the 1980's war on drugs PSA commercial I saw as a kid, where a man is being chased by the police, and it ends with the statement: *"No one says they want to be a junkie when they grow up."*

There is a reason that no one yells out a lot of the jobs that we have. They are not creative. They aren't fun. They aren't sexy. I am not saying that every job must be creative. We need all kinds of jobs—blue collar, white collar, and everything in between—but I am worried that we are not raising the next generation to be self-actualizing.

How many people have you met (maybe it's you) who are a lawyer or an accountant, who secretly or openly hates their job and has a midlife crisis brewing on the horizon? Maybe when they were growing up they wanted to be a ballerina or firefighter, but someone told them it wasn't practical, or they were not good enough, or they'd never make money, so they gave up on their dream.

A dream or hope deferred does dry up, and it makes the heart sick. Not realizing your dreams can lead to depression, unhappiness, and other serious consequences. Australian author Bronnie Ware, a nurse working in hospice, recorded the top-five most common regrets of the dying. Three of them really resonate with me: live the life you want, I wish I hadn't worked so hard and I wish I had let myself be happier.

Live The Life You Want

Ware stated that the most common regret of all is living an unfulfilled life. People spend so much time trying to live the life their parents, family, spouse, kids, or society wants for them instead of what they want for themselves. You see this in the person who is a nurse but hates patients. You ask them, "Why do you do it?" and they say, "It was what you did back then. You got a good job and worked until you retired." Doesn't matter if little Suzy wanted to be a chef; her parents were never going to accept that and let her aspire to be the next Julia Child or Rachael Ray (who, by the way, is not a trained chef). Lissa Rankin says, *"Write the prescription for your life."* If you're not working at a job that is getting you closer to your dream, then quit it and find one that supports your future, even if it is simply a stepping stone and not the final destination. There is no point in living one more second doing something that you do not want to do, or that does not fulfill you, or, as Marie Kondo says, "sparks joy."

When my mom was going through her divorce, it was hard. We came from a strict religious upbringing (pretty much everyone but me became a minister), and it was a big no-no to get divorced. But I gave my mom the same advice I'll give you. You could live another twenty or thirty years—are you going to stay one more day and be miserable? I don't think God wants you to be trapped in something. He says he always provides "a way of escape." If your mama wanted you to marry him, then she can live with him!

I Wish I Hadn't Worked So Hard

This second reflection from Ware is especially important. You cannot be so narrowly focused on self-improvement and your goals that you forgo and forsake your family and your friends and other important aspects of life like your health. No one on their deathbed says, "I wish I worked harder for my boss, or that company I didn't really like, in that job I didn't really care for." But I believe they would be happy saying, "I am glad I wrote that book," or "I am proud that I was a good parent."

Ware found that this statement was said by mostly male patients. I think it is still ingrained in most men that they must work hard. The grin-and-bear-it approach. Many men in the past generation worked for jobs they hated, stayed in them until they got their gold watch and retirement party, only to die a few years after retirement. And on their deathbed, they had nothing but regret for a job they loathed and all the moments they missed with their children. Don't let that be you.

I Wish I Had Let Myself Be Happier

Money does not make you happy, but it can help you to buy things that can enrich your life or bless the lives of others. I believe happiness comes from within, but I believe it is inextricably linked to your inner passion and purpose. If you are in a relationship or job that makes you unhappy, get out. I believe honestly if you work toward goals and see progress, you will be happier than people who are not doing that. I think some people have been trained to think they get what they get and they are supposed to settle for average or mediocre. I believe that is the minimum standard. Don't make that baseline the goal. That is just a starting point.

Our founding fathers said we have the right to life, liberty, and the pursuit of happiness. Happiness must be actively pursued; you must do something to be happy. You must change your mindset and your way of thinking; you must change your attitude and expectations; you must change yourself and sometimes your situation. If you are not happy, the only one who can change that is you. If you live under the assumption that someone or something is going to come along and make you happy, or if you delay your happiness by saying, "Someday I'll be happy," wishing, thinking, hoping, and praying *won't* make it so. Pursuing makes it so.

If You Could Wave A Magic Wand, What Would You Change?

Einstein believed in thought experiments. Take a moment to close your eyes and just envision the life that you want for yourself. For some of you, you will see a bad *Highlights* magazine version of "What's wrong with this picture?" One of these things is not like the other. If you could just wave a magic wand and make the picture you have become the picture you want, or snap your fingers like in Mary Poppins and the entire nursery is magically tidy, what would you change first?

Some of you would like to look in the mirror and be twenty pounds lighter. Others would like to see yourself driving a new car. For me, I envision myself winning a Grammy. When you open your eyes, get out a piece of paper and pen and start jotting down what you want at the top. Then start listing how you could do it. Could you download an app to help? Could you start a new program? Join a support group or network? Could you get a savings account and start bringing your lunch instead of eating out? To pursue my goal, I joined NARAS, the National Academy of Recording Arts and Sciences, and started attending events and networking.

I know it sounds too easy, but in many ways it is. When I started writing this book, I got an online course, made an outline, and then started writing. I literally had no idea on Friday, had an outline by Saturday, and this first chapter was written by Sunday. I saw on Pinterest a quote by

Allyson Lewis: *"Change happens in an instant. It happens the moment you DECIDE to change."*[7]

P90X

I remember in 2016 I decided in an instant that I was going to get into better shape, so I committed to doing a year of the home exercise program called the P90 series (P90, P90X, P90X2, P90X3). My back story is similar to other singers. I think of myself as the Luther Vandross of my group. My weight has yo-yoed up and down. I've tried all kinds of diets in the past: South Beach, Atkins, Keto, Paleo, Primal, Slow Carb, Ayurveda, vegetarian, vegan, and also worked with a personal trainer and had some success but then dropped off. The good thing about P90 is I could do it at home. I did not have to go anywhere, which saved me time. The workout had moderate impact and did not require a lot of equipment. It came with a meal plan that was quite easy to follow, and a friend of mine who was a Beachbody coach let me into his Facebook group for motivation and support.

In a year, I ended up losing forty-five pounds, won five hundred dollars in a biggest loser challenge, and was able to fit into old clothes I had not been able to put on in years. You would think that the decision to make that change was hard, but for me it happened in an instant. I made the decision, went online, signed up, and bought the DVDs. In a few days, I had all the equipment and videos ready to embark on my year-long journey.

I remember doing a visualization exercise with my coach. I had to envision myself losing the weight, fitting into those smaller clothes, doing the exercises at home, and having fun. Was it easy? No. Did I want to give up? Yes. Was everything I envisioned exactly how it all played out? Absolutely not! But envisioning was enough to establish the belief that I could do it, and then by the law of attraction, I did. Like magic, the pounds somehow melted off, and I had the energy to roll out of bed

7 Allyson Lewis, "21 Powerful Words That Will Give You Life Motivation." https://www.lifehack.org/articles/communication/motivation-21-words-that-can-change-your-life-and-3-that-will-surprise-you.html.

at 6:30a.m. and listen to Tony Horton yell, "Stella!" and go through the motions toward building a better body, a better mind, and a better me. (It was annoying and irritating at times, but I liked his enthusiasm and his motto: *"Do your best and forget the rest."*)

The Time Is NOW

There is no reason why you cannot *start* living your best life *now*. The only things you need to make your dreams a reality are a decision and a commitment. We will get to how you start making goals, plans, and gathering other things you need later, but first just make the decision today that you are going to change your life.

No one else can do it for you. The day you realize that there is no Superman, and no one is coming to save you but you, the better off you will be. I heard a joke once that said, *"We tried to start a procrastinator's club, but the meetings kept getting postponed."* Make the commitment today to stop putting off that thing you have been wanting to do but just have not taken any action toward. Inaction, in effect, is a decision and commitment to *not* do something. To make the choice to be poor is based on an inaction toward taking steps to be rich.

Some of you might think I am too black-and-white, or I do not empathize with other people's struggles, but that is not true. I have empathy for people who are stuck and do not know how to turn their life around. I want to inspire those who've had the fight taken out of them, who've been beaten up physically and emotionally to the point that they've been robbed of joy and happiness and do not see a way out.

I recall the story in Victor Hugo's *Les Miserables* of Jean Valjean, a thief who stole two candlesticks from a priest and the law caught up with him. The priest, instead of turning Jean Valjean in to the authorities, told them that he did not steal the candlesticks but was given them as a gift. And what a tremendous gift that was. Not only did the priest give Jean Valjean an escape from a physical prison sentence, he offered an escape from a self-imposed prison of his mind. If you have a poor person's mentality, then you will always be poor. The priest said to Jean, "I am giving you these silver candlesticks so that you can become an honest man." Many think, *If only a benevolent person came by and gave me money to start my business or pursue my dreams*. But the priest gave Jean more than money. He gave Jean the freedom of *no more excuses*. Jean had a legal problem. Fixed. He had a poverty problem. Fixed. What excuse could he invent next? Why couldn't he make the choice to become an honest, decent, contributing member of society? And that is exactly what Jean finally did. He became a very wealthy businessman and even adopted a child. None of that would have happened without the priest's intervention and without Jean finally making the choice to stop making excuses. Like the movie *The Wizard of Oz*, your brain (strategic thinking), your heart (self-love), your courage (boldness), and the way home (intuition) has been inside you the whole time. Jean Valjean had honesty and the know-how inside him to be successful all along, but as long as he took the easy way out (stealing) and kept his eyes on temporary things (bread/candlesticks), he could never see the big picture of being an honest man (a man you can look up to).

As we move into the next chapter, it will become clearer that what the priest did is give Jean a reason to live, a purpose. Becoming an honest man was a calling, something bigger than him, bigger than his struggles and his issues. I believe we all need that to be able to keep going when the feeling to persist has long left us.

Answer these questions

1. If you knew you could not fail, what would you want to do with your life?
2. What self-limiting beliefs are holding you back?
3. What is the first step you can make in becoming who you want to be now?

2.

People Need Passion And Purpose

> *"There is no passion to be found playing small—in settling for a life that is less than the one you are capable of living."* —Nelson Mandela, former president of South Africa

In the fall of 2006, at the age of twenty-three, I did what any self-respecting musician who is aimlessly going through life does: I quit my corporate job and set sail on the high seas as a cruise ship entertainer. I had recently bought a very sleek Acura sports car, and less than a month later, I was T-boned in an intersection by another car, and my precious baby was reduced to rubble. I remember the moment of impact, pressed against the steering wheel with an odd smoke coming from the AC, broken glass all over me, horn blaring, with muffled hearing, thinking quietly to myself, *Am I dead?*

I was dead in a way, and my car most certainly went to automobile heaven that night, but I was not dead physically. Just like many stuck in a dead-end job, I was dead inside with no real passion. My band was in a crisis that eventually led to our breakup. I was in a relationship I needed to get out of too. I needed to get away from it all, and this once-in-a-lifetime opportunity literally landed in my lap. A friend of mine randomly picked me up walking on the street and offered to give me a ride home. On the way he also offered me a job to play keyboards in a new cruise ship band that was set to leave in a few days.

The next day I went into the office, told my boss I was quitting, and never looked back. That was on a Wednesday in California, and I was in Florida by Saturday, set to leave for a four-month stint on Holland

America Cruise Lines, having never previously been on a boat. While on the cruise ship, I was afforded the luxury of only having to work a maximum of five hours a day, which was unheard of in my corporate job. Plus, I did not have to make my own food, clean my own room, or commute to work. I decided to make the best use of the newfound time, without all the distraction of the Hollywood shuffle and romance in L.A. and spent my time off working on my personal development: practicing and writing music, getting in shape, and devouring all the books I could get my hands on.

A Purpose-Driven Life

I looked forward to all the return trips to Florida from the Caribbean to get my Amazon packages filled with books that I would have my mom send me while on the ship. One of the books she sent was an autographed copy of Rick Warren's *The Purpose Driven Life* (my mom has been a longtime member of Warren's church and for many years directed the gospel ensemble; my stepdad was on staff at one time too). There is a reason that book sold over 100 million copies, making it one of the best-selling nonfiction books next to the Bible. Rick Warren's words can be lifesaving, literally: a woman was kidnapped and she read the book aloud to her captor and was eventually released because her captor saw his life choices differently after hearing Warren's words.

There is an adage that says, "*When the student is ready, the teacher will appear.*" I had heard about that book and actually had a copy at one point in my life, but it only sat and collected dust. Back then, I had never had the time to read it, or, more accurately, I never made the time. We all have the same twenty-four hours in a day, but we choose what we do with it. When I finally sat down and opened the book, I was immediately enlightened, feeling that I was not alone and that this man was speaking to my core issues. I had never once thought about my purpose. I mean, I always felt music was my purpose and calling, but this was different. This was having something much bigger than myself to connect to. Purpose is defined by the *New American Oxford Dictionary* as *"the reason why something is created or which something exists."* I am not going to debate or argue evolution if we are as human beings created from a physical or spiritual standpoint, but I do believe that everyone is here for a reason. I think we can all agree that we are here to fulfill some mission.

> *A purposeless, passionless life is not really living; it's existing.*

What Is Your Ikigai (Reason For Living)?

Ikigai is a term that comes from studying the oldest living people on the tiny island of Japan, which has more elderly people per capita than anywhere else on earth. The term roughly translates to "reason for living" and encompasses feelings of joy, purpose, general wellbeing, and balance. It comes from two root words: *iki*, meaning "life," and *kai*, meaning "the realization of hopes and dreams." I first heard the term from a free audio book summary in the Blinkist app of the book *Ikigai*, by Puigcerver and Miralles. The authors believe in the theory that understanding one's life purpose leads to happiness, wisdom, longevity, and vitality and could be the secret to living well past one hundred!

I am not sure if I want to live to be nine hundred like Master Yoda in *Star Wars* and then absorb into the force (but I hope I'm as cute as Baby Yoda at age fifty). It is not just about living, though; it is about living a more fulfilled life with the time we have left. For the Japanese, living in your ikigai means that if you find your passion and purpose through work, you should never retire. Or if you find fulfilment from a hobby like collecting coins, you should never give it up. I meet so many people who stop me and say, "Good for you for sticking with music. I used to play, and I gave it up, and now I am old and wish I had stuck with it." I would first tell them thank you, then remind them it is never too late to start again. I do not know why our society thinks we should give up the things that we love. I was studying abroad in France and met a young Indian guy who told me that he was getting to that age when he had to go home and get married to the woman who was picked out for him. Similarly, I used to work with a Korean guy who said that he loved photography and music but was at an age when he had to quit and get a "real job," get married, and start a family. I understand that different cultures have different societal norms and pressures, but could the Japanese really have stumbled upon the panacea to life?

I believe that people are ready to retire not because they felt they fulfilled their purpose, but because they always hated their job, or physically could not do it anymore, or were forced out by ageism. I do not plan to retire. My goal is to be able to do my music full time, while diversified, and teach, mentor, and consult. I already do all these things to a lesser capacity. If there is breath in my body, I want to continue to be useful and work on the projects that make me feel good.

Years ago, it was common to work for a company, reach retirement age, and then retire, only to die a few years later. What researchers noticed is that people need purpose to continue living. They discovered this in retirement homes, where they gave elderly residents a task to take care of one plant each. The people whom they gave plants to water, talk to, and feed (plant food/sunlight) were found to live longer than other residents who did not have this task. Ruling out underlying health issues, it was decided that the longer life span was due to these people having a reason to wake up in the morning (Rodin & Langer, 1977).[8]

I recall listening to *7 Strategies to Wealth and Happiness* by Jim Rohn. He said you need more to get out of bed and go to work than the reason "I gotta pay these crummy bills."[9] It really is true that if you "make your vocation your vacation, you never work a day in your life." I have had jobs that are soul sucking, and I have also worked in the studio making music for hours and lost track of time. It is so funny how when you want time to go slowly, it seems fast, and when you want it to go fast, it seems like it's taking forever. Too often, people end up working in jobs they hate in order to earn money, to pay bills, and try to impress people who are unimpressed or unfazed and who they don't even like. It is not every day you meet someone who is working toward their purpose, but when you do, you tend to notice they stand out. They are the exception to the rule. These are the people who have taken the time to do a self-inventory,

8 https://www.researchgate.net/profile/Ellen-Langer-2/publication/22550402_Long-Term_Effects_of_a_Control-Relevant_Intervention_with_the_Institutionalized_Aged/links/541175420cf2b4da1bec4ae6/Long-Term-Effects-of-a-Control-Relevant-Intervention-with-the-Institutionalized-Aged.pdf.

9 Jim Rohn, "7 Strategies for Wealth and Happiness," Penguin Random House 1996.

are self-aware, and on their enlightened path to self-actualization. Discovering your ikigai starts by asking yourself four basic questions:

Question 1: What Do I Love To Do?

In the theory of hedonism, it is suggested to seek pleasure and avoid pain; these are the two fundamental building blocks to wellness. It is said when the hormone dopamine releases into our bloodstream, it activates the pleasure center of the brain. Nothing brings a person more pleasure than doing something they love, whether that be biking, hiking, taking a vacation, or talking with an old friend. I truly believe that if you lead a life that is full of things you love, the less anxious, depressed, and worried you will be.

It sounds overly generalized, but can life really be that simple? If you just continually do things you love, will you be happier? I would say no. Life has its ups and downs and challenges, but I feel you are better equipped to face those when your schedule is filled with things you love versus things you loathe. Football Coach Bruce Arians was quoted as saying, *"You can die at any moment doing anything. So why not do what you love to do?"*

It is easy for those of us who have already found our purpose, but what do you do if you don't know what makes you tick, your why, that thing you love more than life itself, that you want to do first thing when you wake up until your head hits the pillow at night? One of the best ways to know what someone loves is to look at where they spend their time and money.

For me, as I look around my apartment at the things I have bought myself and spent the most money on, I see my music equipment, my record player, and my vinyl collection. Of course, I have many other things, like a TV and pictures, and lots of kitchen gadgets and miscellaneous stuff, but it would be very clear to most people at first glance that I am a musician or that music is a great love or passion of mine. As far as looking at my calendar and seeing my time, I see in the past a lot of concerts, practices, performances, teaching lessons, taking classes, and other things that would also indicate music is on the top of my to-do list.

Take a self-inventory of your spending and your calendar over the past month. What did you do the most? What did you buy the most? If you see that you went out to eat five times a week, you may find that you are a foodie. If you spent a lot of time at the gym, you might be a fitness buff. And if you spent a lot of time at the library, you may be a literary enthusiast. What if you could take those things and create something you love? Who better than a foodie to start a food vlog? Maybe that fitness buff could study and become a personal trainer or that bookworm become a literary critic.

This is not to say that you must try to make a hobby or career out of everything you love; you most certainly can go putt-putting without trying to get into PGA championships. It is okay and extremely healthy to do things just for recreation. I understand the frustration of not finding everything you want to do to self-actualize at your nine-to-five job. Most people working a day gig are helping their boss's dream come true instead of working on their own dreams. I believe everyone should have a side hustle or hobby that allows them to explore other parts of themselves and have an outlet for self-expression aside from work.

Some people have allowed their lives to get so hectic, keeping up with the Joneses, that they have lost sight of what they love to do. They have a lot of commitments in their life, overshadowing and preventing them from doing what they love. There are others who know what they love to do but are afraid of being embarrassed or are wary of what people will say. Secretly I have always loved to dance. As I got older, I was seen as a wallflower because I stopped trying to look stupid in public. No one would *really* notice though, especially if they were dancing too. Sometimes we stop ourselves before anyone else has the chance. It is our misguided self-preservation, something left over from our prehistoric ancestors, a fear of being ostracized from the pack.

Some people neglect what they love to do because they feel that they do not have the time. What they fail to realize is that time can be found, just like money. In finance there is something called a dribble or drip account; that is, when you are not watching your pennies, it is very easy to lose them, spending money on lunches out, or expensive lattes, which can derail you from savings goals, such as for a house or car. In the same way, you can have a dribble or drip account from your time bank that is leaking like a sieve, making you lose time. In the same way that in personal finance these accounts are fixed by having a budget and knowing where your money goes, you must also learn to budget your time more wisely. In fact, I believe time is the most precious commodity we trade now, and we barter money for it daily.

You don't have to be a wizard, warlock, or genie to magically create more time for yourself, but you do need to be organized and intentional in your strategy. Blogger and author Jon Acuff, in his first book *Quitter*, discussed how to balance work, speaking engagements, blogging, marriage, a new baby, and writing a book. He gave examples of how he had to start waking up an hour early to get his one hour of daily writing in for the book. He found that he was not distracted when his wife and baby were still asleep, and when the office was closed and no interruptive calls, texts, or emails were coming through. He still had the same twenty-four hours in a day we all do, but he decided to sacrifice one hour of sleep for one hour of productivity. It sounds easy, but if so, why doesn't everyone do it then?

Not everyone is willing to make the sacrifice, and most are not willing to make it daily. Motivational speaker Brian Tracy has said at several of his seminars:

> *"There is an interesting point about the price of success; it must always be paid in full and in advance. Everyone wants to be successful. Everyone wants to be healthy, happy, thin, and rich. But most people are not willing to pay the price."*[10]

I recall when I wanted to get in shape, I had to do the exact same thing as Jon Acuff. I had to set my alarm for 6:30a.m., roll out of bed, and either go to the gym, run, or work out at home with DVDS six days a week, sticking to a rigid diet plan. I knew that after working all day, exercise would be the furthest thing from my mind. I would go out to eat or have a drink or see a band, so I knew my night life would derail my exercise efforts. I quickly realized that no one was going to eat or grab a cocktail or see a concert at 6:30a.m. (at least I hope not). But most people

10 Brian Tracy, "TOP 25 PRICE OF SUCCESS QUOTES | A–Z Quotes." https://www.azquotes.com/quotes/topics/price-of-success.html.

make excuses about working out in the morning even if they want to lose weight. They don't want to sacrifice—they don't want to get up early, put on clothes, and grab those weights. In effect, they want to reach their goal with no effort. They essentially are saying to themselves, "I am not willing to pay the price!"

Question 2: What Am I Good At?

When I would get my report card as a kid, my parents and I would bypass all the As and zero in on the Bs. They would tell me, "You will just have to work a little bit harder to get those grades up." They never said, "Way to go on these As," until I started making straight As (and therein lies my struggles with never feeling good enough and perfectionism). I always excelled in my music classes and several other subjects, but my worst subject was, ironically, gym. I was small for my age, the youngest in my class, and when God was handing out the brains and looks, I got a double portion, but as far as body and physical coordination goes, well ... he must have run out by the time I got in line. I was the kid who could never hit the ball, never climb the rope, and always was picked last for team activities.

I recall in middle school that I started skipping gym and going to extra music classes instead. It was going great until I got my report card and received a D in gym. I remember sitting in the hallways after school, crying to a friend, afraid to go home and face the music. School is made for everyone to follow one path and one set of rules to one destination—graduation. It is built for the compliant and impressionable kids, but most certainly not for the free-spirited ones. We say that no child is left behind, but in fact many of them are every day. Many children who think, feel, or act differently are often either pushed through or pushed aside.

It became clear to me by the end of high school that I knew music was what I wanted to do with my life. But was I good at it? In the beginning, I struggled to find my way. In fact, an old church member told me that when I was younger, I was not very good, and they didn't know why the children's choir director picked me so often for solos (I assume because I was eager and unafraid). But by high school I had gotten much better, and this old church member said that she enjoyed hearing me sing now.

I was in musicals, multiple choirs, piano lessons, all-state choir, and had even won the NAACP ACT-SO (Afro-Academic, Cultural, Technological and Scientific Olympics) competition with a free trip to NYC by the end of senior year. Gym was the least of my worries as I had already fulfilled my one credit in freshman year. (I got an A this time by showing up and powering through.) I could not have cared less about working my physical muscles as much as my brain and music muscles. Because doing what you are good at gives you a satisfaction that doing something you are bad at will never give you.

It Is Okay To Be Bad At First

This is not to say that everything you love to do you will be good at, and most likely, when doing anything for the first time, you may be really bad at it. My early demo recordings have never seen the light of day on Spotify with my other catalog, and for good reason: they are unlistenable. I did not know anything about recording. I was just making what in writing is called a "vomit draft." I was literally spitting out whatever was on my mind at the time. But I always believed that it takes writing through the bad songs to get to the good ones.

Recently I was going through old song lyric notes on my phone and ran across some early lyrics for the lead single "Let Me Down" on my first EP in 2013, *Who the Funk Is Cliff Beach?* I had three different verses and a bridge that died on the cutting room floor, and it was originally in a different key. At the time, I am sure I thought the ideas presented on my notepad were good, but eventually another better idea must have swooped in and trumped those fallen soldiers. I cringe reading them back because they are so bad, but understand that if I never wrote them, I may have never gotten to the right ones that fit the mood of the song perfectly now. Being bad is a part of the process. It is a journey, and a long one, to get to self-actualization.

I am reminded that Paul McCartney dreamed of the tune "Yesterday" and had a process of putting in dummy lyrics that he would later replace. Originally the song was called "Scrambled Eggs." Would this hit song have become the most covered song of all time if you heard the words,

"Scrambled eggs, oh you've got such lovely legs," instead of "Yesterday, all my troubles seemed so far away," blasting from your stereo?

Also, not everything that you are good at is necessarily something you love to do. I have met many athletes who were good at their sport, or musicians who were good at their craft but later ended up giving it up. Their heart just wasn't in it anymore.

But what we are trying to ascertain is what you are good at. It should be amazingly easy for you to quickly jot down a list. Things that you are good at are always top of mind, because people innately gravitate to things they do well versus things they view themselves as doing poorly.

For example, you may be incredibly good at doing research. If I were to give you a random topic like "What should diabetics eat?" then Google would become your best friend and you could catalog, alphabetize, and disseminate more links and parenthetical references on the subject than I would have time to read in one lifetime. You would be good at becoming a fact checker, a research assistant, or librarian, but you would not be necessarily good as an athlete, mechanic, or audio engineer.

A lot of times people realize that they are good at something but have not made the connections to maximize and make that work for them, or find ways to be compensated for the things that they are good at. This is not something taught in school unfortunately. There is no class in Making a Life 101, at least not in any school I've heard of. There are numerous self-help books and life coaches, but not everyone has access to them, and even if everyone were to be presented with inspirational information, it might be more theoretical than practical. To be honest, putting a life together is hard, and not everyone will be up to the task.

Self-Awareness Is Crucial

I learned early in my career these three things: First, I do not like working in music full time if I'm not doing my own music. Whatever I do, I need to be diversified, and I like the stability of working within a structure. I played on cruise ships for almost one year before I came back to dry land and decided to go back to school at Pepperdine University to get my MBA. I felt I wanted to learn more about business, as I think it is the backbone of our society. I was also tired of playing songs that I did not choose, in the style of the recordings—like live karaoke with no room for imagination. Whether they tell you in school or not, you are a business, whether you work for someone or for yourself. This is why so many artists end up getting screwed over by the record company or their accountant—because they are not taught that they are the business and thus need to keep an eye on the details of what is going on in their financial lives.

Second, in business, when looking at any portfolio, whether it be a 401K or assets you own or manage, the more diversified you are the less likelihood that all the assets or stocks/bonds/funds might go belly up. It is best to hedge your bets or spread them out. In my musical life, I am a singer, songwriter, teacher, mentor, producer, arranger, label owner, publisher, and more. In my work life, I handle digital, tech, IT, systems, processes, operations, logistics, strategy, organization, customer service, social media, and more. Whatever it is you do, you will most likely end up wearing many hats. If you, like me, are juggling many things, write them all down, as noted earlier, and circle which ones you are really good at versus the ones you can do but you might not be the best at. Begin to focus on your top three.

Some people are lucky to be good at many things. This can be a two-edged sword though. On one hand, it is great, but on the other hand, like the Cheesecake Factory, there might be too many items on the menu to choose from, so you get analysis paralysis and have trouble making a decision or sticking to something. You must again begin to focus on the top-three things you are good at.

Third, I realized I like working within a structure. I like getting paid on time. I like having a schedule. I like having benefits and perks. I could continue to climb the corporate ladder, but there comes a point when I am working more for them than for me, so I have to always maintain a balance for myself (they will not do it for you).

Some people do not like being in a nine-to-five job; they prefer a more flexible gig-economy job like Uber or Upwork. This is good to know about yourself. If you try to get a classic nine-to-five, the rigidness of it will make you unhappy and want to quit. But if you are like me and you thrive with structure, then having an Uber or Upwork job might not work for you, or you will have to make your own structure to make that work. A structure that works for you is created by trial and error over time and also based on best practices from similar organisations. All things are possible but knowing yourself will help you save time and energy and help you to create the situation that will foster your success and provide your best output.

Question 3: How Can You Help The World?

Think about the impact of what you do. Not everyone is going to become a Mother Teresa or Albert Schweitzer. In business you could become an Andrew Carnegie or in the arts a Bono; there are many ways to help people and change the world. Pretty much every product and service made by a business (just watch *Shark Tank*), excels when helping to solve a felt need. Uber solved the problem of being able to get an affordable taxi ride (and helped drunk drivers not get DUIs). Freshly or Blue Apron helps busy people get food delivered to their home, either prepared or easy to prepare. Airbnb helps people find affordable alternatives to expensive hotels. The list is endless of all the inventions, songs, movies, art, businesses, and technologies created that make our lives a little easier and more comfortable daily.

When you think about helping the world, start small. Maybe you only start working on helping yourself first. This is exactly what Sara Blakely, maker of the billion-dollar product Spanx, set out to do. She started tinkering in her house on a prototype of a product that would make her look slimmer in her work clothes, without being too restrictive like the girdles of the 1950s and '60s. So, she set out to make a product that would help solve the felt needs of millions of women (and some men) who also wanted to look their best in their attire. Did Sara know when she started that she had a billion-dollar idea inside her? Probably not. But I am sure she knew that just by solving that problem for herself, others likely had that same problem, and if it could help her, it could help them too. Then it snowballed from there.

Maybe you will start by changing your immediate sphere of influence. Ralph Smedley, founder of Toastmasters International, originally started out with a few small classes to help young men learn public speaking and leadership skills at the YMCA in Santa Ana, California, in 1924. To date, Toastmasters has over 350,000 members worldwide in over

140 countries and more than 16,400 clubs globally. Do you think young Ralph thought that his classes would eventually become such a juggernaut? Probably not. But he knew the power of being able to communicate effectively in life, work, or education and wanted to impart that skill and knowledge to these young men. He helped where he could.

Harriet Tubman was a slave in the mid-nineteenth century. She was afflicted with headaches and dizzy spells from an early childhood trauma, so it is unlikely that she set out to eventually free seventy enslaved African-Americans, embark on over thirteen trips across the Underground Railroad, be chased by dogs and slave owners, or risk her life to become one of the greatest abolitionists of American history. Originally, she set out to free herself. She is remembered and memorialized every Black History Month for her work in helping end slavery. The women's suffrage movement also esteems her as a role model and trailblazer. Harriet believed all of us have the capacity to do great things. She was not a superwoman; she was just a woman who knew what she had to do.

Where Do I Start?

Starting is always the hardest part. What do I tackle first? Again, the name of the game is to start small. Zig Ziglar, in one of his motivational speeches, told the story of George Washington Carver, an American agriculturalist. He said that Carver asked God to show him the secrets of the universe while sitting under a tree and a peanut fell on Carver's head. God replied to Carver, "This peanut is more your size." Carver, who is now synonymous with the peanut, not only took this divine intervention and ran with it, but discovered 105 recipes for the use of peanuts (and you thought it was just for trail mix and peanut butter). Most intriguing to me is one of the recipes was for peanut milk, many, many years before farmers started producing soy milk and, later, almond, coconut, hemp, and oat milk.

Carver could have wasted time moaning and complaining, pursuing a bigger task, and delaying getting started on what would be his life's work. You, too, may have an exceedingly small idea, but like a seed, if you plant, water, and nurture it, it will grow. And it is important to start now because all good things take time. There are no overnight sensations.

Take the Chinese bamboo tree, for instance. Most trees grow steadily from seedling to mighty oak, while the Chinese bamboo tree seemingly does nothing for the first four years. It does not break ground until after year five. In year five, the tree in just five weeks can grow to be ninety feet tall. But the rub is that you must diligently water and nurture it daily without fail for five years. Do you think the tree magically appeared after five years? Of course not. It was underneath the surface establishing the complex roots it needed underground to be able to sustain exponential growth.

If you want to help the world first, you must get to your roots. You need to be grounded in a solid foundation before you are able to build anything on top of that structure; you would not begin to lay down a foundation without the proper blueprints or a plan. There is a natural law and order to the universe, and you can't circumvent them. You cannot reap in the spring if you did not sow in the fall. And if you plant red tomatoes, you can't pull up white potatoes. In the same way, you cannot help the world if you cannot first help yourself. Similarly, on airplanes, you are instructed in the event of an emergency to put your mask on before helping anyone else. If you pass out from a lack of oxygen, you will not be able to help anyone; in fact, you become a liability.

So how do you want to start helping the world? Maybe you want to volunteer at a no-kill animal shelter. Maybe you want to volunteer to teach financial literacy classes. Maybe you want to play piano at senior citizens' homes. The beauty of this kind of help is that it takes the focus off you and puts it on others. Zig Ziglar's mantra is, "*You can get what you want if you help enough others get what they want.*" I have heard it also said, "*If you want to be a millionaire, help one million people.*" The same rules apply.

Helping people is just one more step toward manifesting your purpose and destiny. I stumbled upon an article by Darren Tong, who identifies four reasons why people procrastinate and do not start or continue on their path to help the world and to self-actualize: 1) anxiety, 2) wanting to have fun, 3) thinking you have plenty of time, and 4) being paralyzed by perfectionism.

Anxiety

Having been diagnosed with anxiety disorder, and having experienced severe panic attacks myself, I understand how anxiety can impede progress and make one slow to start. To a certain point, it is totally natural to be fearful or anxious, especially when starting something new or uncertain. But I have learned over time that as we start doing the thing we are anxious about or fear the most. Usually the anxiety gets smaller or more manageable and starts to dissipate. I am not saying that it is easy. It usually never is, but I am saying that we all have anxiety at times, and the only real cure (not that you should not take medication as directed or as needed) is to face it head-on. Talk about your feelings; they are valid, and it will help ease some of your discomfort.

Fun

When I was a child, the last thing I wanted to do was stay inside and practice my piano. I could see kids outside the window running and playing, while I was moping and sighing, trying to get through my "dozen a day" or "teaching little fingers to play" exercises. I did not find the piano fun as a kid, which is funny now that I am a musician. As a kid, you are not fully formed. You don't know enough to know what you are going to want to do with your life, and you change so much from elementary school to college, so all you can do is start somewhere. Not everything is going to stick, but some of it will.

Plenty Of Time

Microsoft founder and former CEO Bill Gates said, "*Most people overestimate what they can do in one year and underestimate what they can do in ten years.*"[11] Why are people so bad with time? Why do we think we have more time than we think? The fallacy of thinking you have more time is

11 Al Nelson, "Most People Overestimate What They Can Do in One Year" https://medium.com/the-partnered-pen/most-people-overestimate-what-they-can-do-in-one-year-86d44a18b7fa.

cut short when you are confronted with the realization that we are born with a ticking time clock, that death is imminent and inevitable, and that there is no way to escape or get a do-over. With a race against the clock, why aren't we all running all cylinders toward our dreams and goals and aspirations?

I recall when my uncle passed in 2004. I went to the funeral and stayed at his house with my aunt. The house was exactly as he had left it (he died suddenly at home), and I could see home improvement projects left undone, with tools scattered around. I had the innate sense that he likely thought he would have more time to get back to them. Author Mark Twain said it best: *"Never put off until tomorrow what you can do today."*

Perfectionism

I have never yet been presented with a perfect scenario to start. We are human, thus inherently fallible. The world is full of chaos. Murphy's Law is always in effect: *"What can go wrong will go wrong."* Nothing is perfect. You would think that knowing that would be freeing, but many perfectionists cannot let it go. In writing, there is a method called the "vomit draft" (mentioned earlier) where you essentially pour out all your ideas without going back to reread or edit anything until you finish. The reason this is helpful is because it's extremely hard to get out all your ideas in one draft. As soon as you look back, you immediately start to doubt yourself. You think *I could do this better*, and now, hours later, you are still agonizing over the title and have not written one sentence.

Highly successful TED Talk speaker and researcher Brené Brown, in her book *The Gifts of Imperfection*, says:

> *"Perfectionism is a self-destructive and addictive belief system that fuels this primary thought: If I ... do everything perfectly, I can avoid or minimize the painful feelings of shame, judgment, and blame."*[12]

12 Andre Nelson, "The Way of the BA: Dismantling the Ideal of the Perfectionist." https://medium.com/swlh/the-way-of-the-ba-dismantling-the-ideal-of-the-perfectionist-5a13c8da19df.

Perfect is an ideal or standard that no one can live up to; so we must learn to live with imperfection and move into acceptance. You are human. You will make mistakes, and bad things will happen that are out of your control. But a person is not measured by how many times they fall. They are measured by the fact that they got back up.

Question 4: What Can You Make Money Doing?

I think this is the most important piece of the puzzle that many readers are still trying to figure out. If you have a current side hustle or are looking to start one, from a home-based business to a new song, movie, book, podcast, or blog, be reassured that figuring out how to monetize is a struggle for lots of people. First, realize that in working toward your "10,000 hours," as Malcolm Gladwell wrote, to become proficient in whatever it is that you do, you may not make any money from it at first. This is called "paying your dues." If you want to become a public speaker, you will give tons of free speeches; if you want to become an actress, you will do a lot of free parts to build your reel.

But let's say you have already put in your time and paid your dues; how do you start making money today?

Be Careful What You Pick

Some things you love to do and are good at will be difficult or impossible to make money from. There was a lady on *Ripley's Believe It or Not* who could dislocate her eyeballs from the socket. It was a great novelty, and she was good at it, but the likelihood of turning that into a Fortune 500 business was slim to none. You have to know how much money you want to make, and if you want to appeal to the masses like a McDonald's or Starbucks, or serve a specific niche like Lane Bryant (catering to plus-size women) or Big & Tall (catering to plus-size men). Both are fine places to start, and from there you can decide your strategic path.

I have been a part of NARAS, which produces the Grammys, for several years and I have had the pleasure of voting for members who have won Grammys of their own. They have found a lot of success by picking a lane and sticking with it, and usually it is a lane that has fewer people. I have seen people win for Best New Age, Children's, Blues, and other lesser-known categories. If they tried to compete in the larger Pop, R&B, or Rap categories, it would be hard to cut through all the competition and white noise. So, I believe most of us will find and exploit some niche and not go with the masses. In any event, if you go too niche, it becomes so esoteric that you won't be able to have enough of a market to make money (although it is possible in certain academia or in the case of Paul Simon's *Graceland*, which mixed Pop and traditional African music, and gained mass appeal).

What Is Your UVP?

On the Shopify blog, they break down how to figure out something called your Unique Value Proposition, or UVP, and how to market yourself to your niche. Again, this takes us back to having self-awareness. This is where what you love to do and what you are good at and what will help benefit others comes into play to help you figure out how to make money from this business idea, product, or service you want to offer. The UVP can be around price (like Walmart), demographics (like FUBU), quality (like Patagonia), psychographics (like TOMS Shoes), or geography (like In and Out).

Conscious consumers, for example, is a concept I deal with a lot in the beauty industry. With the expansion of information technology, customers are much savvier when it comes to ingredients; many want gluten-free, natural, organic, vegan, or cruelty-free products. They want a company that also has good values and gives back to the community. They care about the environment and how they can effect change. We saw this with the recent boycott of Chick-fil-A (around LBTQ+ issues) and how Popeyes and other competitors responded (on Twitter, clucking back), with Popeyes taking market share with their almost un-gettable chicken sandwich (planned with beanie baby-like scarcity).

The first thing you need to ask yourself is: *What is the demand for what I do? Is it high? Is it specialized? Do I have a lot of competition? Are there a lot of barriers to entry?* If you are thinking of starting your own social media network to compete with Twitter, Facebook, or Instagram, then I would say that unless you have Amazon or Apple backing you, don't waste your time. Now, if you told me that you are starting a new online community for pet lovers and you have Petco and other brands interested, then I would say hop in your car and get to Silicon Valley as fast as you can, cause you just might have something.

How Are Others Monetizing?

One of the most fascinating industry phenomena that baffles me is what I like to call the Water Wars. How did bottled water become a thing? Water is pretty much everywhere in the developed world; you can get it right out of the tap at any time. But sometime in the '70s there was a rumor that tap water was no longer "good" for you, and sale of bottled water slowly started to rise. Large beverage companies like Coca Cola and Pepsi started to buy up all the water companies and enter the market, against leaders like Perrier, Evian, and Arrowhead. Then you had people saying that plastic bottles were no good for you and the water inside was no good, which gave rise to new technology like Pur faucet enhancements and Brita carbon filters. I tested out water from an expensive alkaline machine by Enagic, which makes "Kangen" water. Somehow, many genius businesses were able to figure out how to monetize a commodity that is literally all around us.

How can you view others doing what you do or want to do and see how they monetize it? Years ago, the only way to join a profession was to be someone's apprentice. They would mentor you and in return get cheap or free labor in the hopes that you would take over the business when they retire. Some people in college do internships, and in the medical profession you must still make the rounds, but in most jobs now, you learn on the job.

If you want to be a mechanic, I most certainly would go find one whose work you admire and try to work under them and learn that craft. Learn to ask insightful questions, find out how they got started, what they did differently, and their tips, tricks, and wisdom will be gold to you. In business school, it was quite common for us to schedule information interviews with people working in our field. With social networks like LinkedIn, it is extremely easy to find someone doing what you want to do and message them. The days of privacy almost do not exist. You can find almost anyone's email on their website or some type of contact information on their social media in order to get to the top CEO of any company by a few degrees. This is an important first step in making new moves within your career.

What Would You Want More Than Money?

Not everyone who wants to live within their ikigai is concerned about money. There are other ways to measure success. In the musical *Rent*, famous for a song "Seasons of Love," the composer Jonathan Larson wrote "525,600 minutes, how do you measure a year? Measure in Love." That would be great, right? Gather around, arm in arm, singing "Kum ba ya?" But there are many things that are measured not in money but just as fruitful and rewarding.

Gaining a new skill is invaluable. You cannot put a price on that. Billionaire investor Warren Buffet has no degrees on his walls at Berkshire Hathaway, just one certificate in public speaking from the Dale Carnegie School. Could he measure that like he could his net worth? Not quantifiably, but qualitatively he could. In fact, Buffet told *Inc.* magazine that public speaking is the "one skill that can boost your career value by 50 percent."

When I was starting to learn the piano, I had no idea that it would lead to me making money as a performer, teacher, and songwriter, nor what it would teach me about discipline, creativity, and delayed gratification. *National Geographic* released an article stating, "Your aging brain will be in better shape if you take music lessons." It won't turn an ordinary kid into a genius, but it can give your brain a lifelong boost. Whether I ever made money from it or not, what it did to my developing mind is priceless.

Some people believe money is the root of all evil, but I am here to tell you that it is not. Ask anyone who has been poor and gone hungry, and they will tell you it is better to have money than not. Money can't buy you happiness, but the lack of it can make you very unhappy. It is true it is not everything, so assuming you have enough to cover your basic needs, you can actually take the time to do things you love and are good at that do not necessarily make you money but could lead you to making money in the future.

I help people all the time and never get a dime for my help, and I am sure you are the same way. How many friends have you helped move (free moving company)? How many call you to vent (free therapist)? How many pick your brain for advice (free consultant)? You should start charging your friends, no? Friends are not clients. But some of those skills could translate into money; you can still measure their intrinsic value. Being a good friend is its own reward. It's the same as being a good parent. You will never get paid for that; in fact, you will pay a lifetime of money, time, and tears, and it is a debt that your kids can never repay (they are liabilities and are entitled to support and care). I recall my mom always singing to me Shirley Caesar's "No Charge" with the line, "for the nine months I carried you, no charge," explaining to her son all the sacrifices she had made for him his entire life. In the same way, there are many government services and charities that will never make money.

What is more important to you than money? I believe health is wealth. In 2019, I was diagnosed with three illnesses I could have for the rest of my life, which were reversible if caught early, or they could be managed by making some lifestyle changes and taking three medications. You cannot put a price on good health. Ask anyone who has lost someone to cancer or anyone suffering with a long-term illness. They would pay anything not to have a disease nor to have lost a loved one.

Time is more important than money. I gladly pay my maid to come and clean so I can have two hours to go do other things. (I also hate cleaning.) I pay to have food delivered so I can do other stuff instead of cooking. All types of other paid services exist to free up more of our valuable, precious time. Brian Tracy, in his book *Time Management*, says, "*You should delegate everything that you possibly can to other people to free up more time for you to engage in your 'A' (your most important, or most lucrative) activities.*"[13]

Back to Larson's statement about love. No one wants to die cold and alone, like the end of the movie *Titanic*. You want to die at home, surrounded by the people who love you the most. A life without love is very tragic indeed. The poorest person is rich when they are loved. There is

13 Brian Tracy, "Time Management", AMACOM 2014, p.37

not enough money in the world to make someone love you who does not. Even in the story of Aladdin, the all-powerful genie could not make two people fall in love (though Cupid can, but it isn't true love).

So, we clearly see that it is okay in life to enjoy doing something, and it can be your ikigai without making a dime from it. You can still proactively measure its effectiveness in other ways. I love to walk outside. I walk thirty to sixty minutes a day for health, both mental and physical, but you will never see me as a competitive walker (Google the sport racewalking). That does not mean that I do not see the value in it. In fact, self-care is one of the most important and valuable things you can do, and it will help you tackle your other money-making schemes.

What Happens If You Don't Do It?

Elizabeth Gilbert, author of *Eat, Pray, Love*, believes that ideas are infinite and will come to you from the universe like magic, trying to get your attention. Sometimes you will not notice, usually from preoccupations and having a busy life. But when you are still and quiet, you may notice and decide, "No, thank you, I am just too busy to act upon that idea." And what happens to that idea? Does it die with you? No! Gilbert believes it will float back into the universe and go to someone else. How many times have you seen something on TV or read somewhere about a new invention or product or service and thought, *Man, I have been thinking about that idea for years and someone else finally made it?* How many of you could have made Netflix or Uber or the Snuggie? (Is that still around?) But in the moment when you had that idea you either said no, or were distracted, or never noticed, and someone else plucked it up and ran with it.

You cannot go back and cry over spilt milk. Other ideas will come to you, don't worry. But you should take the time to think about the consequences of inaction. When starting to write this book, I learned that everyone fears they have nothing original to say. To put your mind at ease, in these types of prescriptive nonfiction books, nothing is truly original, but the authors should still write them. Why? Because I believe no two people are alike. Even if it is the same idea, or the same information going through you, it is a different funnel, filter, lens, or conduit, and the exact outcome will be slightly different. In music, so many songs use the same chords, and in the end we all have the same twelve notes, but I still love hearing new interpretations of them every day.

Also, you must see that unrealized potential can wreak havoc on the mind, body, soul, and spirit. It's similar for your ideas or dreams if you keep them locked inside and never do anything with them. It breeds the cancers of depression, regret, disappointment, shame, blame, and sadness. None of these sound like what you want, but your inaction is a crime against your own interests.

In law there are instances when a failure to act could rise to the level of criminal liability. If a doctor doesn't help a sick patient or a lifeguard doesn't save a drowning victim, someone could die or suffer physical harm and the professional could be criminally prosecuted, convicted, and jailed. In the same way, not acting on your dreams and aspirations, locking them away inside you, is effectively putting yourself inside a prison of your own choosing. Nobody wants that.

We know from hospice workers that many die full of regret and unrealized potential. I have heard many thought leaders say that the graveyard is one of the richest places in the world. We have lost those ideas. If you were to die without pursuing your dreams, how many songs, movies, books, inventions, services, products, and scientific, medical, and technological breakthroughs might the world be robbed of because you did not carry out the ideas the universe sent your way?

You are waiting on the world, while the world is waiting on you. Air Jordan Shoes are a multi-billion-dollar product sponsored by one of the most successful sports stars, Michael Jordan, and produced by the world-renowned shoe company Nike. When first approached, Jordan was a Converse fan and favored them over Nikes, which he never wore. Jordan's mom had to persuade him to take a meeting with Nike and, even then, he still declined, until Nike offered him five times what Converse offered, and he signed the deal. Jordan eventually bit the bullet. As the Nike slogan says, he had to "just do it," and the rest is history. According to *Forbes*, Michael Jordan made over one billion dollars from Nike Air Jordans, the biggest endorsement deal in sports history.

What if Jordan didn't do that deal? Could it have been Magic Johnson or Scottie Pippin or someone else instead? Very possible. A lot has to do with serendipity, luck, divine providence, and timing, but the world will never know.

As you start to really think about your life in terms of your ikigai, what you love to do, what you are good at, what the world needs, and what you can make money doing, now you have to start thinking, *If I don't do these things, what money and opportunities could I lose, and what is the impact on the world if this does not happen?*

When you start to think about life in these ways, you are starting to think about yourself in the same way that I do as a business consultant to small businesses—helping them to think about how they should approach business when rolling out new products and services. You are evolving from just You to You, Inc.

Answer These Questions:

1. What are you good at?
2. What do you love to do?
3. What does the world need from you?
4. What can you make money doing?

3.

Restructuring You, Inc.

> *"No matter how much or little a company pays, your name matters more than their name. Build your Brand."* —Olawale Daniel, author, *10 Ways to Sponsor More Downlines in Your Network Marketing Business*

Having my MBA and working for a Fortune 500 company, I spent many years helping companies find a way to solve problems by making incremental and large-scale internal changes. As a result, I've learned that we need to treat ourselves like a business—trim the fat, scale, and have a mission statement and vision.

People Perish For Lack Of A Vision

The Fred Hollows Foundation at hollows.org has created an online sight simulator that demonstrates what it is like to be legally blind. Using Google street view, you can search an address and then use a slider to change the severity to simulate the effects of cataracts, glaucoma, or diabetic retinopathy. Having type 2 diabetes and having had a great-grandparent who died from it has made me take strong action to get it under control. Diabetic retinopathy is the world's leading cause of blindness, and anyone with diabetes is at risk. The best cure is early detection (visiting the optometrist annually, taking your meds, being proactive). For those of you without diabetes, this may not be a worry to you, but I am sure that you can imagine what it would be like to wake up blind, unable to clearly see the world around you.

As I virtually walked through the online simulator, at the greatest severity I could make out only faint shapes and colors. Everything was a blur. When I removed all severity, I was viewing Alhambra, California, and was able to recognize several restaurants outside of an Edwards Cinema. Sometimes in life we take things, like our health or our senses, such as eyesight, for granted. If you lost your eyesight, how much would you be willing to pay to get it back? Anything? Everything you had? You would quickly realize that vision is priceless.

Making A Statement

Laurie Beth Jones is an internationally known, best-selling author. In her book *The Path*, she discusses the importance of having a mission statement for your work *and* life: *"A purpose statement is a written-down reason for being. Clarity is power: Once you are clear about what you were put here to do then 'jobs' become only a means toward accomplishing your mission, not an end in themselves."* A mission statement should be short, succinct, and so easy to remember and understand, even a child could understand it.

HubSpot, on their blog, catalogs some of the best mission statements from various well-known companies and foundations. Here are some vision statements:

> **Microsoft** (at its founding by Bill Gates in 1975): "... a computer on every desk, in every home."
>
> **Alzheimer's Association**: "A world without Alzheimer's disease."
>
> **Disney**: "To entertain, inform, and inspire people around the globe."
>
> **Facebook**: "Connect friends and the world around you."

Mission and vision statements, though they go hand in hand, are actually quite different. A mission statement is what you stand for now, while a vision statement is where you are headed. A mission focuses on the task at hand today, and vision is where you ultimately want to end up. I believe, though, at your core, your values should remain consistent. They are the DNA and lifeblood of your work. All three are important and vital to organizations and people.

Simon Sinek taps into this when he suggests that you "start with why." In his 2009 TED Talk, he popularized this term, having studied business and thought leaders. He believes the brightest futures come from leaders who think, act, and communicate differently than their competition; by discovering their "why," they find more clarity, meaning, and fulfillment in whatever they do.

But what is *your* why?

You must let your inner child speak—yes, that annoying, inquisitive, insatiable voice that would tire out your parents. The one that asks, "Are we there yet? Are we there yet? Are we there yet?" or "But why? But why? But why?" As a professor's research assistant in college, I learned: "*to get the right answer, you have to start asking the right questions.*" You need a strong why to get out of bed. When you hear your baby crying in the middle of the night, you awaken and run quickly with a bottle or a diaper in hand because you know your why. When they slip and fall, and you run outside with a Band-Aid, ointment, and peroxide, you know your why. But when your boss is yelling at you at a job you hate, after you have sat in traffic to get there, and then customers are also screaming on the phone, do you know your why then? I wasn't sure myself until I started asking myself, *Why can't I be more, have more, do more? Why can't I figure it all out? Why can't I succeed?* And then I realized I could, but it all started with taking baby steps.

Start With Small Changes First

I feel most fulfilled if I can do one thing per day that will help move the needle on my several side businesses and creative endeavors. Motivational speaker Les Brown said, *"Shoot the moon, and if you miss you might hit a star,"* but fish in a barrel are a much easier target. I took part in a New Year's resolution challenge once; we were supposed to mark the time when we started, and then note when we completed it or gave up. Most people gave up almost immediately after starting because as soon as they failed once, they packed it all in. This happens often in life, which is why I believe, even though I am a high-achieving person, that I do not set the bar too far out of reach. In theory, I underwhelm myself. Setting the very achievable goal of doing one thing fulfilling for myself per day is a target anyone could hit. I do not even qualify it by the amount of time or level of impact. It is simply a one-to-one ratio. If I send an email, that counts. If I practice, that counts. If I take a class, that counts. If I teach, write, perform, produce, or arrange, that counts. If I balance my books, or book a show, or schedule an interview, or write a chapter, that all counts. Some of these things take a few seconds, like texting a colleague; some take months or years, like securing a contract. Whatever it is, I guarantee you will find more success if you have this one-a-day method. It works for vitamins, so why can't this be your success pill?

A decade ago, I was trying to pay off credit card debt after just finishing business school. It was the middle of a jobless recession; I was sleeping on my best friend's futon, being sued by all my creditors and harassed by collectors. My car was broken down and about to be repossessed. I felt like an immense failure. At that time, I discovered a contrarian out of Nashville who had lost it all, too, and learned a different way of living. In fact, he "lives like no one else, so he can live like no one else." Radio personality and author Dave Ramsey has helped millions of people get out of debt by going through what he calls "the baby steps." I volunteered for many years teaching at Financial Peace University and was able to clean up all my consumer debt and then help others do the same.

The first step in Dave's system is to save $1,000 as a starter emergency fund. To some this may seem like nothing, but to others it may be more money than you ever have had in your savings account before. The reason for this figure is that you are supposed to work toward this goal very quickly, in the first few months. The psychology behind this is that there is something enormously powerful that happens when you achieve a goal. Poet Maya Angelou said, "*They may not remember what you said or did, but they will remember how you made them feel.*" I say all the time that "there is a special feeling inside that comes from finality." Finishing something, finding closure, is immensely powerful. When I saved that $1,000, I still owed my creditors, but it gave me the feeling that I could, through hard work and perseverance, make it through this life- altering situation.

Not everyone subscribes to Dave's radical methods or way of life, and some consider his methods controversial, but that does not mean it is not sound. Baby steps make a whole lot of sense to me. You must crawl before you walk and walk before you run and train before you run a marathon. If you come into any given situation, overwhelming yourself with an all-or-nothing ultimatum to succeed or die trying, the moment you fail once, you will be sidelined. The other reason why I like the baby steps analogy is that when babies learn to walk, they fall many, many times in the beginning, but they are pretty much unfazed. Falling is part of the learning process. They just pick themselves up and start all over again and again and again until finally they are running so fast their parents can hardly keep up with them. You've never heard a baby say, "Oh man, I'll never get it right. I might as well just sit down and never try again." This mostly happens because we usually learn to walk before we talk (so you can literally walk the walk but not talk the talk), and they also do not know any better. Babies do not know the meaning of failure, and so they have inherent optimism. They see all their falls and failures as temporary and immediately get up and try again. And that is exactly what you will have to do.

Slow And Steady

Often, people want to use a microwave for something that belongs in the crock pot. Good things take time. I have been working on my craft for almost twenty years. And I, like my other colleagues, am still in the trenches every day. Nothing is handed to us; we must claw and work at it. In the fable *The Tortoise and the Hare*, for all intents and purposes, the hare should have won. He was much faster, but he was also foolish. He underestimated the tortoise, who was terribly slow but very methodical and diligent in his approach. Poet Henry Wadsworth Longfellow has a notorious line from his poem "The Ladder of St. Augustine" that reads:

> *"The heights by great men reached and kept were not attained by sudden flight, but they, while their companions slept, were toiling upward in the night."*[14]

14 Henry Wadsworth Longfellow, "The Ladder of St. Augustine".

My dad used to summarize this point: "Once you stop, that is when another man surpasses you." I inherited my mother's strong work ethic. Now I know that starting small can eventually help you gain tremendous momentum and lead to larger-scale changes.

How Do You Eat An Elephant?

When setting out to devour an elephant, even the biggest snake unhinging its jaw would not dare to try to take it on whole. You would have to eat it one bite at a time. In the same way, if you have big goals, you would have to take them on in bite-sized chunks.

I worked previously for a Fortune 500 company, one of the largest in the world in the beauty industry. Post-acquisition of the company, I was tasked to lead the change management of our Enterprise Resource Planning System and our website platform. We had to migrate both systems at the same time and there were a lot of moving parts. To break it down:

- We had to be educated and train on the new system.
- We had to train others in this new system.
- We had to migrate our legacy data into the new system.
- We had to create new processes.
- We had to make updates on the back and front end.

It seems like it would be straightforward, but as soon as I got deep into it, I could suddenly feel the heat of the internal friction and the effect of new constraints. I had to stay dedicated to the task throughout. You cannot lose fidelity. We could not simply put up a "Closed for Maintenance" sign to make the switch; we had to make sure customers would never experience any disruption in services. What I did not realize is the psychology of the buy-in and the complexity of merging existing teams together into a new ecosystem.

People resist change. Let's be honest. The devil you know is better than the devil you do not know. We are all a little distrusting of what is new; that is why most of us are late adopters of new technologies. How many times have you been in a work meeting when someone says, "But that's not the way we've always done it before"? I am sure Tower

Records and Circuit City yelled that as their empires came tumbling down like the walls of Jericho all around them too.

Change is constant, and change is inevitable. And those who do not learn to adapt and press forward will get left behind. I believe I was prepared for the task of leading this change-management team because I got that point:

- Left D.C. for Boston
- Left Boston for L.A.
- Moved out on my own
- Left my corporate job to entertain on cruise ships
- Left cruise ships to get my MBA
- Pivoted into a new industry (beauty, which I knew absolutely nothing about)
- Started teaching myself e-commerce (a new skill)

I had other large life changes, and I am sure you must too. My point is there will be times in your life and career where you will face large, difficult changes in building and improving You, Inc. But remember it is You, Inc., not You, Ink! This means nothing is set in stone. Write your life in pencil not in pen. If you make a mistake, get your eraser out and start over again. As author and cartoonist Stephen McCranie said, *"The master has failed more times than the beginner has even tried."*

Unburying My failures

I did not set out to write a book to make myself look good. I am not proud of everything I have done. I have failed way more than I have ever succeeded, and I have the battle scars to prove it. I already told you how I lost everything and was sued by everyone. I started two books I never finished before this. I had several relationships that did not work out, jobs that I was fired from, and businesses that did not take off. I am not worried about any of that, though, because I feel that is all part of life's journey. That is how we learn—by doing, by making mistakes. I don't know why people want to try to be perfect; we know it is humanly impossible, and yet we try to do it anyway only to be disappointed when we fail miserably.

I currently work at a small beauty firm and we have pivoted many times in the months I have been there. The nature of the business and the landscape of retail has changed so much with recent current events. Everyone is scrambling to figure out where we go from here. I have tried to add in multiple types of software that did not jibe well with our system. I have overpaid for shipping by mistake. I have set erroneous codes, emailed the wrong person, and made several other mistakes, none of them life threatening, but mistakes nonetheless. Every failure is a lesson. A teachable moment. When your kid comes to you with her tail between her legs, sheepish, to tell you the wrong she has done, try to listen and understand that you have made mistakes, too, and you have the chance to allow them to learn and grow.

It is too bad we fear making mistakes. Our lizard brain, the part where fight-or-flight lives, wants to avoid pain at all costs. Mistakes can be extremely painful. Ask anyone who has cheated on their spouse and gotten caught. Most feel it was a mistake and have tons of remorse and regret. We, at our core, if we are good people, do not set out to ruin someone else's day, week, month, or even their year (that wouldn't be being a good friend). But sometimes, even with the best intentions, we make mistakes. You, Inc., like any other company, can fail at any time. Just like all the companies that were too big to fail, like Toys "R" Us or Washington Mutual Bank, pride leads to a painful, pitiful downfall. You can avoid some of these mistakes and pitfalls and learn a better way to lead small- and large-scale changes by creating a board of directors or advisors for yourself.

Advice Is Free

When starting my record label, I knew I wanted to pick the brain of someone who had done it before. I had interned at a few labels in the past but did not keep in touch with the management and, due to high turnover, I had lost a lot of contact information. So, I decided to enlist SCORE to help me gain the business insight I needed. SCORE is a national nonprofit organization that offers resources from the Small Business Administration; it consists of volunteers who are expert business mentors, some retired, some still working, but all are ready to help people who are involved in young businesses with education and mentorship.

I am based in L.A., and the only label owner I could connect with through SCORE was based in San Diego. We would have weekly phone sessions followed by a string of email threads. I was in fairly good shape, according to her, but it was still great just to get the guidance and reassurance. She had a label that produced classical music; my label produced soul music, so we had no conflict of interest and everything said in SCORE is kept confidential, so I felt comfortable discussing the details of my business concerns.

I really enjoyed and benefited from our chats. After a time, I did not need the mentorship anymore, but I have recommended SCORE to many in my Toastmasters and Masterminds groups, because this type of free help is invaluable.

Why would you not learn from someone who has already done what you want to do and is farther up the road than you? I have been a mentor to many musicians over the years, and it is hard but rewarding work. Seeing them take the stage at places like The Wiltern to perform in front of screaming, adoring fans, get write-ups in *Billboard*, or tour domestically or internationally, is a great joy. Their success is in part my success. I didn't do it for fame or notoriety; I did it to give back to the artist community in which I am a part and that I love.

In the beauty industry, I still keep in touch with my old boss, not just for glowing recommendations, but because he is always continuing to grow and improve himself and is happy to share some nuggets of truth with me.

The goal of an advisory board for a company is to bring together a body of people who can give strategic advice to management. This is different from a board of directors, as the advisors do not have a vote or say in your business but are there to guide you to make the best decisions for yourself. The main reason for creating an advisory board is to get outside ideas, to see things from an outsider's perspective. In You, Inc., your emotions can often cloud your objectivity; you are too close to it and having the input of others provides a fresh way of thinking. Even when we do work with partners or peers, it is still extremely easy to fall into groupthink, so having fresh blood helps to avoid this scenario.

You may not have to go far to see you already have a great group around you—and they can become your advisors too. Maybe you have a parent, another family member, friend, or a work colleague who can join your team. Maybe you can turn to a teacher or a coach. One of my best mentors is an old college professor. She not only taught me how to think for myself, but to research and ask probing and insightful questions. She helped shape my academic approach to lifelong learning, and I will forever be changed and immensely grateful. Where can you start to find these great people?

But sometimes you may not know anyone whom you think could be helpful, so you might have to cold call or email people or reach out via social networks like LinkedIn. And sometimes you can get great advice from books, master classes, webinars, or whatever you have access to. The point is to start thinking about where the information you need is and how you can get it.

One biblical proverb states, "*Fools despise wisdom and instruction*" (Proverbs 1:7 NIV). I know that no one wants to knowingly be a fool. It is also said that fools rush in. Developing You, Inc., requires time and attention to avoid the possibility of crashing and burning quickly. You owe it to yourself to ask for help early. You would be surprised how many intelligent people are readily available to speak with you and share their knowledge. They can give you great ideas to help incorporate structure and order to any chaos you might be experiencing.

Your Organizational Structure

Organizations, like the human body, are designed to have a certain structure to run as smoothly and efficiently as possible. Even the smallest company of one is compartmentalized into an owner (executive decision maker), a finance/accounting department (budget handler), receivables (payment collector), marketing (promoter), production (product or service worker), customer service (client manager), human resources (employee advocate), R&D (new idea generator), and sales (product and service pitcher). Let's break down each one:

Owner: This is the person who sets the mission, vision, and overall strategy for the company. They are responsible for the entire business. They are the one in the hot seat and liable if something goes wrong.

Finance / Accounting: This person has their hands on the purse strings. They help to balance and stick to the budget and make sure the company stays in the black.

Receivables: This person collects all the money owed to you.

Marketing: This is the person who dreams of ways to promote your product, service, and ideas to your target audience.

Production / Operations: This is the person doing the leg or grunt work. This person provides the actual service.

Customer Service: This is the good cop who makes the customer/client feel heard and special. They answer all the correspondence. They help keep the existing business happy.

Human Resources: They make sure you are taken care of and can help bring in new hires as the business needs to change and grow.

R&D: They research and develop new ideas and improvements.

Sales: They nurture the existing business prospects and find new work through networking and referrals.

If you have never thought of yourself as a solopreneur (working for yourself) in this manner, you really should start. You probably do not currently realize just how many hats you have been wearing.

Some of you are probably thinking this is overwhelming or that all these departments are not needed to run a successful You, Inc., but you would be wrong. It does take preparation to create your organization, and for some of you who thrive in chaos, this might seem like unnecessary work. But I will give an example to hopefully make things clearer.

Every year, come tax time, if you have not kept your receipts properly, you will have to spend an exorbitant amount of time to get everything together to either do your own taxes or meet with your tax professional. If you are using QuickBooks or some other type of software for billing and invoices, and if you are also tracking receipts and tagging them properly for easy retrieval, then you are way ahead of the game. Among the small business owners I know, this is often not the case. I attended a webinar recently, hosted by Demir Bentley of the Lifehack Method. In a poll among participants, almost 90 percent do not pre-plan their week. I am in the 10 percent that do. This is a necessary step in being more productive and getting more things done, just like organizing the structure of You, Inc. This is going to save you time, and you will have fewer headaches in the future. We all have the same twenty-four hours in a day—someone else is just using theirs more efficiently than you.

Writer Marisha Pessl says it best in her debut novel, *Special Topics in Calamity Physics*: "*No wonder so many adults long to return to university, to all those deadlines—ahhh, that structure! Scaffolding to which we may cling! Even if it is arbitrary, without it we're lost ... in our sad, bewildering lives.*"[15] I learned this during my brief time of unemployment and when I was working from home. My best days always have some type of structure, even if loose. I like to have a working idea of how the day should go. Yes, I schedule my downtime. And why is that? Because when I didn't, I could not run my life; instead, it ran me. I was always running out of time or not getting things done or someone was throwing some grenade into my day, whether it be work or play, that would keep me from accomplishing the things that I wanted to do most. When last unemployed, this was my schedule for a typical day:

9:00: Wake up and go for a morning walk.
10:00: Shower, then get dressed.
11:00: Eat breakfast.
12:00–2:00: Seek work opportunities.
2:00: Eat lunch.
3:00–5:00: Work on my side business.
5:00: Work on music.
7:00: Engage in social activity and eat dinner.
After 10:00: Enjoy downtime, TV, and reading.
In bed at midnight: lights out by 1:00 a.m.

15 Marisha Pessl, "30+ quotes from Special Topics in Calamity Physics." https://bookquoters.com/book/special-topics-in-calamity-physics.

If I did not keep a schedule as if I had a job, I would have been in a worse predicament because I would have been aimlessly going through life with no target. Unemployment is a time to make finding your next job your job, and to get things you have put on the back burner onto the front burner. Some people feel guilty with too much free time. As a result, anxiety, depression, and worry set in as money dwindles, and they start to lose their purpose. Having a structure during this time is one of the only things that got me through. I am not saying that my exact structure will work for everyone. Even if you do not stick to it completely, just having a loose structure in place gives you a frame of reference. Knowing You, Inc.'s structure will help in identifying any gaps or farming out dreadful work to someone else so you can focus on your most urgent tasks.

When To Hire Someone

In the beginning, unless you married rich or inherited great sums of money, you will be a one-stop shop, doing everything yourself for your business/personal project until your side hustle is generating enough income or worth the investment to hire someone else. In the early days, I did everything I could on my own and had a lot of friends do favors for me to get my music career jump started. I did not have a lot of money so everything took more time. Previously, I was blessed with a friend who invested in my project and parents who donated to my cause, but for the most part I have always been self-funded. I have had many friends who were successful in crowdfunding their project; but after having an investor, I realized that I did not want to accept money from anyone who would try to influence how the records were made. I wanted 100 percent artistic freedom and control over all personnel. I also never wanted the liability of owing someone money or products hanging over me and, luckily, I have not been in that situation. It was easier, even if it took longer, to put skin in the game with my own time, money, and sweat equity.

I believe it truly takes teamwork to make a dream work. I am often reminded of Dorothy in *The Wizard of Oz*: I picked up my own Tin Man, Scarecrow, and Cowardly Lion as I made my way down the perilous yellow brick road of my music career. The first hire I added on was my PR agent. I have had several PR agents and still employ two as of this writing. Having a publicist, if you can afford one, is a must. People need to know that you exist. But I still do a lot of PR work myself and have been able to land spots with several key outlets, for example, CNN, completely on my own.

I have also had success using a tag-team approach. The next person I added to my team was my booking agent. I have an agent based in Las Vegas who has been great at expanding me into other markets. My agent has connections that I do not have, and it is nice to have another person working to find great venues. The agent helped me get a spot on Fox News and arranged for me to play shows on and off the Strip, including my first Ticketmaster event at Rio Vegas. I have had several licensing agents who have come on board to pitch my music and have had great success in adding on a radio promotion team, specialized to my genre, who have helped me get on dozens of stations across the country, most recently KCRW. The final piece to my puzzle was adding distribution for my records and record label; the last company to come aboard covered physical distribution domestically and globally for the physical, vinyl records for *California Soul Music*.

Did this happen all at once? Of course not. I had to leverage contacts in my network and make a lot of cold emails and calls to be able to build these partnerships over a period of three years. But I have a full-fledged indie record label now, ready to sign new acts, and push out more of my music too! Was it difficult? Yes, painstakingly so. Lots of playing the waiting game, hoping someone would listen to and like my stuff, to take a chance on working with me. And I am quite sure that you can find yourself in this same place. So how do you do it?

Proof Of Concept

You need to quickly make some type of tangible medium of your work to show what you can do. For me, it was making my first EP in 2013. By then, I had songs out and could send them to people to listen to via links—that was my proof of concept. If you want to be a chef, you can do the same by perfecting a few dishes and have your friends test them. Record and document on video your process, and let people download the recipes from your website. That way, even if no one knows who you are, you can easily send a PDF or links to YouTube videos showing you know what you are talking about. If you want to earn money as a writer, start with making a short e-book that people can download for free as a PDF to read, or start writing your own blog or podcast, and try to secure some freelance writing jobs with that proof of concept, sending links to your website blog and podcast for them to read and listen to. If you want to be a tax accountant, go through a course at H&R Block or a similar company and do a season of taxes for them; then volunteer to do some friends' taxes as your first clients. You need to make your intangible ideas into something tangible—concrete. Making them tangible makes it more real to you and everybody else. In fact, for music you must document your song in some tangible form, writing it down or recording it to be able to copyright it. An idea in your head will stay in your head and have no real value until you take that idea from the realm of possibility into the realm of reality.

Plan Of Attack

I believe you can have everything, but not all at once. Tucker Max, who runs the Scribe Course for Writing, which is helping me to write this book, says that if you try to have it all at once, you'll end up with a "meatball sundae." Meatballs are great and ice cream is great, but they are not great together. You cannot put everything you want and need into one basket. Again, unless your last name is Kardashian, money is finite and so are your resources. That is why you are working a side hustle while simultaneously working your full-time job. So, you will need a plan of attack to prioritize who you hire first. Depending on what you are trying to do, this list will be different for each person.

For me, it started with self-awareness. To be able to get things done musically, I know I play only two instruments: I sing and play piano. I knew if I wanted to perform with other instruments (not using synthesized or computerized sound), I was going to have to enlist others—and I did. My music is more organic; plus, I learn so much from all my players in my ten-piece band. I am not a recording engineer, so all my recordings are done by ProTools whizzes and mastered at great studios in California, with people who have the expertise and sensibilities to get it done. Could I have learned these skills? Maybe. But I would not tune my own piano or fix my own Rhodes. I do not have the time or patience, and I prefer to field this work out.

For you, make a priority list of who you need first. If you are a writer, you need to start thinking about an editor, publisher, or agent. For someone who wants to teach a course, you need to start thinking about online education platforms, universities (onsite or distance learning), and textbook publishers. For DJs, you need to start thinking about clubs, venues, radio stations (physical or online), and agencies. For almost any side hustle/gig economy work, there is a clear, direct line to the "who" you need to build, grow, and support your business. Google will be your best friend, as well as your social media connections. If you are a busy person, you may want to think about a virtual assistant, intern, or other service to help free up your time, which we will discuss more in the Delegation section later in the book.

Budget

Once you have identified who you need, you will need to figure out the feasibility of hiring your team. For me, paying for PR is always an upfront cost (to my dismay), so I know that will impact cash flow immediately, but it is a necessary evil in marketing my product. Booking and licensing agents instead charge you percentages based on what they "kill" and bring to the table, with no upfront cost, making them easier to bring on board. So, with both of those you can have as many as you like if they are nonexclusive. For distribution, you pay for the product up front, but they pay you for that product to sell to their clients in a B2B situation. Of course, you carry inventory risk, so I like to get pre-orders before producing, if possible.

But you might not have any money right now and may be in need of some help. Maybe you have a spouse, friend, or loved one who can help, or maybe you can hire an intern. Some of you have money from your main job (this is my method); just make sure you are thinking through your priority list and looking for cost savings wherever you can. I have bartered and bargained a lot over the years, and it has been the only way for me to get some things done under budget. There are some people I would love to work with who are out of my price range, so I keep them in a "wish list" pile that I can build on later. Always start where you are today, and try to be patient. It will take some time to find the right mix that works for you.

Portfolio Management (The Wheel Of Life)

I was extremely fortunate to stumble upon the concept of the Wheel of Life a few years ago. It is a tool often used by life coaches to give clients a bird's-eye view of their lives. I took the free assessment on Noomii.com. I suggest you try it out for yourself. It really is eye-opening. Just like a business would manage its assets portfolio, similar to a stock portfolio, by diversifying, you want to make sure you try to remain balanced, as it is very easy to get off balance juggling a full-time career and your side hustle(s).

The Wheel of Life tool varies from site to site, but I like to boil it down to these five sections: Love/Family/Friends/Community, Fun/Entertainment/Recreation, Money/Career, Health/Wellness/Fitness/Self-Care, and Spirituality/Religion. In this book, we are focusing mostly on Money/Career, but I hope some Fun comes from the work that you do. Later, I will discuss self-care. It is all about balance. There is no way you can have the energy and mental stamina to work your side hustle effectively if any sections on the wheel are neglected. I have seen many achieve a lot only to have risked their health and now must take time off from their career and spend money to fix that. So, even though we will not deep dive into all five sections of the wheel here, they are equally important. Let's look briefly at how they work together in your side hustle journey.

Love/Family/Friends/Community:

> This is your support system. This is your personal network and, often, your first clients (or guinea pigs). There is nothing worse than getting to the top only to look around and not be able to share that moment with anyone you care about or who cares about you. They knew you before the success, fame, and fortune, so they will help to keep you grounded.

Fun/Entertainment/Recreation:

My side hustle, music, is rewarding and often fun. But in this instance, I'd like to talk about things I do that are not related to my side hustle. I listen to music for recreation and entertainment, or I go see shows, but I also like to read, listen to podcasts, cook (but hate to clean), travel, and watch TV or binge Netflix. These activities help keep me sane, providing me with some downtime and rest, which has always been hard for me. But rest is where we find *rest*oration; the body and mind repair themselves. I am finding it more important as I get older. You cannot just go, go, go on all cylinders all the time; you will either burn out or blow out.

Money/Career:

On the Wheel of Life, this is where people include side hustles for money, unless it is a hobby like coin or stamp collecting, in which that would fall under recreation/hobbies. This is also where your nine-to-five full-time job goes. Budgeting, saving, and investing all fall into this category as well. I believe at least half of our time is devoted to this sector. Without money, almost everything else is impossible. "The best things in life are free" is good on a bumper sticker or sound bite, but money makes the world go round. If you are in a dead-end job you hate or that is taxing you, knowing this information helps you to push even more deeply into your side hustle or look for new employment that you can enjoy.

Health/Wellness/Fitness/Self-Care:

As mentioned earlier, in 2019, I was diagnosed with type 2 diabetes, high blood pressure, and high cholesterol—on top of a previous diagnosis of fatty liver disease. The word *disease* literally translates to *not at ease*. I was so busy working my day job and working on my side hustle to pay proper attention to my health. Drinking alcohol, eating fast food, and not moving nearly enough, my body was left with no choice but to tell me to slow down and change some of my bad habits. I cut out a lot of sugar, salt, and all alcohol, got an Apple watch to track my steps, and committed to walking thirty to sixty minutes every day. I enjoy the time outside, and my numbers remarkably improved over the first six months—with the help of some medications as well. I also started doing guided meditations, taking baths and showers to relax, getting massages, and visiting the chiropractor weekly. This is just a part of the maintenance of my mind and body.

Spirituality/Religion:

I grew up in a Christian household, so spirituality and faith are near and dear to my heart. I have found that in the storms of life I have an inner calm that others around me do not seem to have. I do not ever say that one form of religion is better or worse, but I have most certainly seen people who seem calmer than others for many reasons, and I attribute this to spirituality. I read a lot on the subject and listen to sermons. It brings me great comfort and joy. I pray and meditate. I have known others who chant, utilize the healing powers of crystals, and do other things that I respect. It is important to find what works for you and keep it as a daily practice.

Brand U

Whether you have a business or are just representing yourself, you must learn that you are being marketed and that you are a brand. When you look at a celebrity like J.Lo or Beyoncé, everything you see that is public-facing, even candid shots, are pretty much all staged. They are the by-product of the juggernaut marketing machine behind them. Most of you do not realize that deep inside you there is a "uniqueness," a product of your personality and experiences, and people are craving to connect with you; they just may not know it yet. How is your brand doing? How do people see you? What kind of first impression do you make in person and online?

I learned, after several failed attempts, to start really focusing on my brand. For my music career, you will see I am dressed in red and black 99 percent of the time. I took my branding idea from the White Stripes, who wore red and white (which they took from peppermint candy). You will see this on my album covers, in the clothing I wear, on social media, and live; these colors are in my logo, it is my brand DNA. For my record label, California Soul Music, we made the logo to represent the Cali lifestyle and laid back music scene, with gold and blue hues, and a record replacing the sun, with swirls in the letters to represent ocean waves. There are marketing companies that specialize in helping people figure out how to best represent their brand publicly. You might have heard the terms "on brand" or "off brand" thrown around. You must decide what your brand is. Let's look at a few brand logos that represent the thorough process behind this business strategy.

FEDEX: The E near the X is purposely created to form an arrow pointing right, which signifies they are pushing you forward with their logistics and technology.

Amazon: The arrow in their logo is going from the A to Z, showing that they literally have everything you need, while paying homage to their bookseller beginnings.

Baskin Robbins: The ice cream behemoth used pink in the B and R in their logo to reveal 31, which is pointing to the number of flavors offered in their ice cream shops around the world.

I am sure there are dozens of other cases where companies have used great branding and marketing to create a subliminal message that, when we start noticing it, we can clearly see is intentional. In the same way, you will have to take time to think about how you represent yourself, by your style and wardrobe, photography, products, services, and copy (what you say and how you say it).

Malcolm Forbes personified what it means to create a brand: "*Too many people overvalue what they are not and undervalue what they are.*"[16] Branding is making a statement about what you are. But to do that you

16 Andrea Cordray,"Too many people overvalue what they are not [...]" https://www.umw.edu/lcpw/2019/05/02/too-many-people-overvalue-what-they-are-not-and-undervalue-what-they-are-malcolm-forbes/.

have to define what you are not. McDonald's delivers the same quality and service all around the globe. But they do not deliver the best hamburger ever made. There is a difference.

To continue with this example, you need to understand that McDonald's knows its target audience, that is, people looking for reliable, cheap, fast food. They have built a foundation for this over sixty-five years. They have an irresistible proposition—that you can get the same product anywhere in the world. They have created systems and controls in their organization to make this possible. It may be called different names, a quarter-pounder versus a royale with cheese, but it ultimately tastes the same. (I have had it in America and France, and it is the same, although, doctor's orders, I would not eat it now.) They have a website that carries this message (not sure how much this helps *them*, but *you* will need one). The message is also in every location and commercial. They have a clear content, visibility, and delivery strategy. They foster a community, with Ronald McDonald Charities and Play Places for kids and families (a true "Happy Meal"). Their strategies are similar to what you will have to create for your brand. Branding is how the world sees you. Zappos is a brand that is known for great customer service and is now a billion-dollar company. Your first impression is crucial; taking the time to think through your branding can be a key to your success.

Reviews

Getting feedback is a valuable part of building your business profile. In Toastmasters, every meeting has a section for evaluations, where speakers can receive feedback about how to improve their public speaking. This is one of the few organizations I have been in that does this well, often using the sandwich approach (giving a compliment, then criticism, then a compliment) to make the feedback easier to swallow.

I love getting feedback. If I give speeches in a vacuum, then I will never know if I am improving. You can learn how to tailor what you want to say to what your audience needs to hear. We often think we know what is best, but the end user or customer is the one who wants to use or enjoy your product or service.

For some of you, getting feedback may be difficult, especially as a solopreneur, but it is not impossible. You can always poll your friends to give you an honest opinion. Restaurants have feedback cards; companies have email and social polls. Some companies employ market research firms to invite focus groups to give feedback on their product or TV show. There's a joke in marketing that you can make the best dog food ads, photos, and commercials, but if the dog won't eat it, then the owner won't buy it. Don't waste your money marketing something without getting any feedback on how the customer would like it. Take the time to get feedback before you invest money in your product only to end up with tons of inventory you can't sell or an office space you can't afford.

I recall interning for a record label that had a CD they were selling for a lot of money because it came with video content they thought was unbelievably valuable. But the content was already available for free on YouTube so, as a relative outsider looking in, I said, "Why would I pay double for the CD to get a DVD of material I can see on YouTube? Why not just unbundle and let me buy the CD for half the price?" I could offer that feedback because I was not emotionally or monetarily attached to the decision, whereas the decision makers were.

Author Ken Blanchard said, "*Feedback is the breakfast of champions.*" People often get offended and emotional when it comes to feedback. I am an advocate for tact, and sometimes the truth can be tough to hear, but it's better to rip it off like a Band-Aid now than have to suffer more later. I welcome feedback. I want to improve. There is no way that I will become better or survive without it. The purpose of feedback is to understand your strengths and weaknesses. Knowing your weaknesses can help you gather people around you who have strengths in those areas and who can support you. Coach Doc Rivers said, "*Average players want to be left alone. Good players want to be coached. Great players want to be told the truth.*"[17] Do you want to be average or do you want to be great? Left to your own devices, you always only know what you know, and I can tell you now that you do not know everything; it is impossible. Your mind would explode like Jim Carrey's Riddler. If you want to be good, you will

17 Kim McCullough. "Useful Motivational Quotes" Hockey Weekly, vol. 42, no. 13, Hockey Weekly, Feb. 2016, p. 15.

take some advice and coaching, but I believe that is only going to get you so far. To be great you must get comfortable with the truth. You have to, as Brené Brown advocates, "Get vulnerable."

Vulnerability sucks. When you are exposed and are open, the truth can cut like a knife right through the bone and into the marrow of the soul. Say a doctor comes in and tells you the truth that you have cancer. Does that truth suck? Yes, it does. But what if you did not have this information and then become very ill or die suddenly because you didn't know and could take no action to prevent it? Now, what if they tell you, "We caught it early and, with the right course of treatment, you can beat it and live for many, many years to come." The truth, though tough, would come with action steps to improve and get better. Feedback is information used to improve. It should be emotionless, but we are human and fragile. I try to conduct business as emotionlessly as possible, but as an artist it can be exceedingly difficult. Some of you will have an easier time than others.

At a nine-to-five job, at least in the corporate world, you usually have, at minimum, an annual review. Most people just listen to see if they will receive a raise (I know I do), but these check-ins with management or your direct reports, if you are a manager, are a good way to gauge how things are doing. I think a lot of times we leave things unsaid, thinking that the person knows it. It is great to be told verbally that you are doing a good job. When I was in customer service, getting feedback that I was helpful to a customer really made my day. In fact, I would keep printouts of the best ones to review whenever I had bad customer experiences. Getting cursed out as the manager of escalations, I looked at these and my affirmations almost daily.

In my music, I have a press section on my website where I get to read all my positive press highlights. I like to print pictures of these and have them around the house to look at on those days where I feel like Sisyphus: damned for all eternity to push a boulder uphill only to watch it roll back down again. I cannot remember if the rock falls on the other side and he has to run down and push it back the other way, or if it rolls back over him and crushes him, but in any event, it is his own personal hell. Of course, the feedback cannot always be positive.

I used to love watching film critics Gene Siskel and Roger Ebert on

TV as a kid debating about movies that I had not seen with words I could not understand. One thing was clear, if they gave a movie two thumbs up, people were going to see it. But the most interesting shows were when they disagreed. One gave a thumbs up and one gave a thumbs down. They would have a knock-down, drag-out fight as if they were not friends and colleagues, as if they never knew each other, thinking how could the other possibly be so stupid as to love or hate this film. It was great television, even if I was not their prime audience. I could hear the passion in their raised voices and knew that they were knowledgeable on the subject. But in the end, no matter how heated they became, they calmed down and stayed friends. The criticism was just information, and sometimes you will agree with it or not. Of course, film criticism is more of an art than a science, more opinion than fact. But the point is, feedback still is crucial and critical to any business, and having scheduled reviews, even if by yourself, and taking an inventory of how things are going, will be immensely beneficial.

Answer These Questions:

1. How can you run your life like a business?
2. What departments in your life are underperforming?
3. How can you fix those underperforming segments?
4. What drastic changes are you willing to make?

4.

Start Yesterday Or Today But Not Tomorrow

> *"Most times, the way isn't clear, but you want to start anyway. It is in starting with the first step that other steps become clearer."*
> —Israelmore Ayivor, author, *Leaders' Frontpage: Leadership Insights from 21 Martin Luther King Jr. Thoughts*

When I was starting to write my first book, which was a bust, I had the pleasure of going to Zig Ziglar's company to interview his son, Tom. Zig was my great motivational speaking hero. Tom agreed to meet with me, signed a copy of the last book he and his dad worked on together, and showed me around their HQ, where I got to see the famous "golden water pump." "Prime the Pump' was one of Zig Ziglar's most popular speeches. You must prime the pump by adding water in before you start getting water back out. The moral is you must always put something in (time, money, energy) before you can get something back out. That moment solidified for me one of the points that Zig Ziglar made: *"You don't have to be great to start, but you have to start to be great."*[18] Some ideas have never even seen the light of day because people do not know where to start. If I never started writing then, I would not be writing now. I have found that we fail to start mostly out of fear—that we will fail or look

18 "Soundbites" *Journal of Property Management*, vol. 79, no. 6, Institute of Real Estate Management, Nov. 2014, p. 7.

foolish or become paralyzed by analysis paralysis or procrastination, waiting for the perfect situation or someone else to come along to help us.

Seven years ago, I sat down and stared at a blank Microsoft Word document and began to list the ideas of what I wanted to create musically over the next decade. This is a document entitled "Who the Funk Is Cliff Beach and Beyond," which I have saved on my old external hard drive. In it, I laid out the groundwork of songs that would be on my first two EPS, my first full-length album, and several other works. Although the document has changed several times over the years, I made many of those records. In fact, since 2013, I've made two studio EPS, one studio LP, two live EPS, seven singles, twenty podcast episodes, multiple music videos, a TEDX talk, and a web-based MasterClass. I have been featured on BET, CNN, Fox, and several other media outlets. None of this would have happened if I had not started putting something on that Word doc.

Dare To Dream

Take a piece of paper (or open a blank document) and start dreaming about what you want to do. When I wrote down that I wanted to make ten albums in ten years, I knew I had written a lot of songs between 2006 and 2013 and would write more, but at that time I did not have all the pieces to make that dream a reality. I had no studio; I had never made an album on my own; and I barely had a band of musicians to play with. Before I had ever watched or read *The Secret*, I believed natural universal laws were still at work. The law of attraction, the ability to attract into our lives whatever we are focusing on most, helped me to make that dream come true. By writing down even just the initial sketches of what I wanted to create, I was able to start materializing it. Seeing the goal in your mind is the first step.

Next, I had to start telling people about what I wanted to do. Not everyone I knew—just a few people I could trust to provide support or ideas. There is not one project that I have done that did not require the help of someone else. As I said earlier, teamwork makes the dream work. There are no self-made people. At some point a mentor, client, business, bank, or investor must come along and help you. Even if you are independently wealthy, you do not make, accumulate, or keep wealth in a vacuum. You are the leader, though, for better or worse, so if your project does not get finished, it is on you. You must manage and motivate your team to succeed.

It's All In My Head

The worst thing you can do is keep a plan or idea all in your head. Inadvertently, you will forget something or drop the ball; it is easy for our thoughts to get scrambled. That's why writing things down is important. Your ideas instantly become more tangible and real, which raises the likelihood of follow-through. You are establishing that you are serious about your goals and that they are important.

Unfortunately, I had to learn this skill as an adult. You will not learn it in our current educational system. Brian Tracy studied goal setting for many years and discovered that research shows "less than 3 percent of Americans have written goals, and less than 1 percent review and rewrite their goals on a daily basis." Writing down goals not only helps to better outline what you want to do; it allows you to choose and possess the kind of life you want to live. If you fail to plan, you plan to fail; you are essentially making the choice by not making the choice.

Does anyone succeed without a plan written down? Rarely, and that usually is a very small subset of people who are very lucky, who have other people involved, or who were so mentally diligent they had a plan committed to memory. If this is your first time embarking on this task, write down your ideas as a rough draft to start. It is a living document that will be changed often as you zig and zag along your pathway. And as Brian Tracy alluded to earlier, this should be revised daily.

There Is No Perfect Situation

I have worked on several personal and professional projects, and I cannot think of one that was 100 percent perfect. If you are currently waiting for the perfect opportunity, deal, or situation to occur, I would not hold my breath. Life is too complex to not expect a curveball or monkey wrench to be thrown into your situation. Even with the most adequate planning, trying to think through every contingency of Murphy's Law, there will always be something that you do not anticipate.

Not long ago, I suffered an unexpected job loss but was fortunate to be able to file for unemployment and take some time off to job hunt and work on my music. You would think that since music was not making me enough to live on, I should not have dived headfirst into a new recording project and PR campaign. But I had saved money from a previous severance package and thought this was as good a time as any to invest in myself. That ended up being one of the best musical decisions I have made in my career. I could have put the project off and not spent the money, but ultimately the best investment you can make is in yourself. If I had never done it before, it would have been a gamble, but I had already had several music projects under my belt, and this was one I had a gut feeling was going to be special.

I embarked a year ago on a journey working on a song called "Confident" with Mestizo Beat that led me to two Global Music Awards, a John Lennon Songwriting Grand Prize Award, an amazing video shot on Venice Beach, and over 600 thousand streams as of this writing on Spotify—thanks to inclusion on the All Funked Up and Funk Drive Playlists! Some would say luck had a lot to do with it; I would agree, and I don't think that you do things just to have this type of success. But I also believe if I had shelved that project because I was not in the most ideal situation, none of that success would have been possible. Always remember that good things can grow in crap. What once was waste can become useful fertilizer to your dreams and aspirations.

The Stories We Tell

Let's talk about the stories that we tell ourselves, how we see our situations, how we frame them, and how that can keep us from starting. I spent time studying the psychology of success and learned a lot about psychologist Martin Seligman and his work on learned optimism. The words we say have a direct impact on our lives. The Bible says words "are spirit and life." In an article in *Psychology Today*, Seligman states, "When we say for example, 'It's impossible for me to lose weight,' our behaviours rise up to support this belief, creating a craving for ice cream, leading to overeating and indulgence." But he goes on, "What if you said instead, 'I can make healthy food choices.' That could also be your story and one that would contribute to positive action."

I have learned as an adult that we should challenge our assumptions and beliefs constantly and make sure that what we hold near and dear to our hearts is serving us well. Zig Ziglar tells another story in his talks about how his wife, Jean, always cut off the ends of a ham to prepare it for cooking. He asked Jean, "Why do you always cut off the ends of my good ham before cooking it?"

To which she replied, "I dunno; that's how my momma did it."

So, they called Jean's mom, and Zig asked, "Momma, why do you cut the end of the ham off before cooking it?"

To which she kindly replied, "I dunno; that's how my momma did it."

So, they three-way called Grandma and asked, "Grandma, why do we cut the end of the ham off before cooking it?"

To which she replied, with puzzlement in her voice, "I dunno why y'all are doing it, but I did it because my roaster was too short!"

This humorous story only goes to show that sometimes we have a learned behavior that actually does not make sense for us in our current situation. But the behavior has been passed down generationally, so much so that it is ingrained in us to believe it, and we have no idea why we believe it, only to realize with new information that the belief is false.

I personally *believe* that having a can-do attitude and writing down your ideas on paper pave the best step forward into your future. As I've said, writing down ideas is easy for me, but I realize that for others, staring at a blank page can be a little intimidating, especially for the first time. Try starting by answering these questions from speaker Jim Rohn:

- What do I want to do?
- What do I want to be?
- What do I want to see?
- What do I want to have?
- Where do I want to go?

For this book project, I rhetorically answered:

- What do I want to do? *I would like to write my first book.*
- What do I want to be? *I want to be a writer/author.*

- What do I want to see? *I want to see my finished book printed and retail ready.*
- What do I want to have? *I want to have the tangible version of my book in my hands.*
- Where do I want to go? *I want to go to other cities outside of Los Angeles to promote and discuss my book.*

Jim Rohn says, "*These five questions will define where you're going in life.*"[19] I think that is the whole reason to read this book. To learn to map out where your life is going and course correct, if need be, while enjoying the journey as well as the destination. You will want to answer these questions to begin to start.

Don't Wait

The one thing in life we can never get back is time. I have realized that from previous stolen moments and wasted years in the past. In life, there are no do-overs, but there is regret. Here is an example about the opportunity cost of waiting instead of starting as it relates to saving for retirement. When learning about the miracle of compound interest, the best time to start investing for your future is when you are young. USAA (United Services Automobile Association, a Fortune 500 financial services company) made a chart in 1994[20] (when I was twelve), showing how much money you could have at retirement at sixty-five if you invested $250 a month starting at different ages (assuming an 8 percent average return). If you start at:

Age 25: You'll accumulate $878,570 by age 65.
Age 35: You'll accumulate $375,073 by age 65.
Age 45: You'll accumulate $148,236 by age 65.

---

19 Jim Rohn, "These 5 Questions Will Define Where You're Going in Life ov" 2016 https://www.success.com/rohn-these-5-questions-will-define-where-youre-going-in-life/.

20 Kathleen Elkins, "These 4 charts will totally change how you think about saving money," Sept. 2017 https://www.cnbc.com/2017/09/27/nerdwallet-charts-show-the-power-of-compound-interest.html.

In short, the longer you wait to start, the less you will be able to put away for your retirement years. You can clearly see that each ten-year delay cuts your savings to less than half. Can you start later in life and still be successful? Sure you can. Just look at Colonel Sanders or Grandma Moses. But the only way you can do that if you are middle-aged or above is through more effort on your part. In this example, every ten-year gap would require you to put more money into an account, trying to catch up, and even then, you would have less time for your portfolio to grow. It is doable, but every day you wait, it becomes exponentially harder. As Ben Franklin so aptly put, "You may delay, but time will not."

Some people thrive in the "last minute." They need the stress and anxiety to get things done. But what if they started earlier? How much more could they get done then? You could use this approach by having tight deadlines; then it would feel like last minute but be well organized, but why cause extra stress? I like a very calm, methodical, relaxed approach myself, but to each their own. In either event, a job well begun is half done. The hardest parts of any job are starting and finishing.

Finish What You Start

I could write a whole chapter on starting, but I would be remiss if I didn't mention the value of finishing what you started. How many projects have been started that never get done? In our ever-changing world, with rapid-paced technology and tons of other distractions, it is now easier than ever to not finish. Finishing requires momentum. The biggest killers to our momentum are the constant interruptions.

According to a *Fast Company* article, Gloria Mark, professor of informatics at University of California Irvine, says that we are interrupted nearly every three minutes, and roughly half of these interruptions are self-imposed. Why is this? Joseph Ferrari, author of *Still Procrastinating*, concludes from his research for DePaul University that "nearly one-quarter of adults around the world are chronic procrastinators."[21] He further

21 Jane Porter, "Why You Can Never Finish Anything And How to Finally Change It" https://www.fastcompany.com/3025757/why-you-can-never-finish-anything-and-how-to-finally-change-it.

notes that chronic procrastinators must first realize: "*You can't manage time. You manage yourself.*" So, if you are having a problem with sticking to schedules, or meeting deadlines, or finishing projects, you do not have a time problem, you have a "you" problem.

One of the best ways I have heard to combat constant interruptions is to have a specific time to check and answer emails, or to put your phone on do not disturb mode. Start building a habit to follow-through, which starts with underwhelming yourself. Setting easy goals, you can hit your goals without breaking a sweat and then increase your load. If you want to start eating better, just change one meal a day. Have a salad every day at lunch. That is a low-bar change you can easily do. Then maybe start walking thirty minutes a day, and so on, slowly adding more tasks, and you'll start to build and keep the new habits. If you mess up or miss a day, you have tomorrow to pick it back up.

I've learned that once people mess up, they give up completely, but that is not the best practice. Just like there are no perfect situations, there are also no perfect people. You need to give yourself grace and allow yourself to fail forward. For instance, if you are trying to eat more healthfully, three or four salads out of the week are better than none. Maybe next week you can do five. Schedule a cheat day so you can have some wiggle room. If you make your goal or project too confining, that restriction can end up feeling like a noose that makes it hard to breathe and you will cut it quickly and slip back into your old bad habits.

You must change old routines too. When I stopped drinking alcohol, I stopped hanging out in bars as frequently. If I kept my normal bar schedule, the likelihood of my having another drink would be high. If you are trying to lose weight, you may need to change your typical routes to avoid every fast food restaurant in town. Instead, you might consider heading toward your local gym and then toward the healthier food options. If you want to have different results, then you must do different things. It is the only way. Do whatever it takes to set yourself up for success to start and finish well.

If You Don't, Someone Else Will

Sometimes the best approach can be to think about the inverse or the negative relationships of not taking action to do something. If I had not gone on a blind date, I would never have met my current girlfriend. If I didn't take a chance on the dating app, I would not have had the blind date. And so on. I am sure you can apply the same hindsight in your own life. Now start to look at it with foresight. What are the consequences of not acting toward your goals or dreams? They will never happen, or the likelihood is very slim. You must try first in order to even have the possibility of succeeding.

How many ideas have you seen and said, "Man, I thought of that years ago," and now your idea is staring you in the face? How many of you thought of Uber, Netflix, or Door Dash first but didn't act on those ideas? The people who created these things not only had the idea but the follow-through. I am sure many of us have thought, couldn't *x* be simpler if *y* existed? I probably have more ideas than I will ever be able to execute in a lifetime, and not every idea needs to be executed, at least by you. But if there is something deep inside you have always wanted to do but were too afraid, or lacked time, focus, or commitment, you owe it to yourself and the world to at least try.

There is no runner-up for the Nobel Prize; there's no such thing as second place. This means you must be the first to try and succeed in your field. Is it easy? No. But if you don't try, you'll end up with regret, that nagging *what-if* question. What if I had done this instead of that? What would have happened? I believe most of what is holding us back is fear.

If we do not try, then we have no risk of failure. I believe we have a deep-rooted fear of failure, because no one wants to be criticized or to look foolish. But what if you could make something cool? What if you could do it without the fear of failing? If you could not fail, what would you accomplish now? That is a question my therapist often asks me. Once we eliminate that fear, then we can start to eliminate other obstacles and excuses that are holding us back. We need to take the pressure off ourselves. Yes, it will be scary. Yes, it will be challenging. Yes, it will take up time and resources. But it can also be often fun, valuable, and rewarding too! And again, you will never know what is possible until you try.

Have you ever sat around and wondered why some people have better lives, better careers, or better relationships than you do? Is there some secret? Some magic? Some luck involved in having these things? I think not. I am from a school of thought that if one person can do it, anyone can. This is what is called the Bannister Effect. Roger Bannister was the first athlete to run a mile in under four minutes. Up until the early 1950s, this was deemed physiologically impossible. It was thought that running a mile in that short a time would require such physical stamina that you would die or be seriously injured. But this was disproven in 1954; once that happened, miraculously, another person beat Bannister's record just forty-six days later. Why? Because one person proved it was possible, so others now had a beacon of hope to look toward to see it could be possible for them too.

You can have a better life at any time. I know because I hit rock bottom and then started climbing my way back up. The itsy-bitsy spider did the same thing too. He climbed and he climbed, then the storms of life came and knocked him down. But then the sun came out the next day and dried-up yesterday's obstacles, and the spider began his ascent again. I think this is because spiders do not have developed brains; they don't overthink things. Ants are similar. Jim Rohn explains that if an ant is headed somewhere and you try to stop it, it will look for another way out. It will climb over, under, or around any obstacle. Ants know where they want to go (usually toward food), and they won't let anything stop them. I have seen footage in which ants can band together to create a bridge to get from point a to point b in midair. An ant brain has 250,000 brain cells, and the human brain has 10,000,000. Ants also only live forty-five to sixty days on average versus 27,375 days for humans. We have more brain power and longer lives, yet we don't even think as sharply as an ant to figure out how to get around our own problems to maximize all the extra time and potential we've got!

What if you only had forty-five to sixty days left on earth? In the song "Live Like You Were Dying," the songwriter explains how the main character starts living his best life, since he knows he has only so much time left. We do not know how long we will have on earth. Our time can be cut short in the blink of an eye. Did you know that the people who are most successful realize this and make sure they get the most important things done as early as possible in the day?

What Successful People Do

An article in the *Huffington Post*, entitled, "This is when successful people wake up,"[22] summarizes that 90 percent of executives wake up before six a.m. on weekdays and nearly 50 percent of self-made millionaires wake up three hours before their workday begins. The study also describes what they do before they start working. Many check emails, have coffee, exercise, walk the dog, read the news, meditate, eat breakfast, shower, get dressed, and take the kids to school. The article's author, Andrew Merle, strives to write stories about adopting "good habits for happiness, health, productivity and success." One way to think about why others might be ahead of you is that they have adopted better habits than you have.

Aristotle said, "*We are what we repeatedly do*." Excellence then is not an act but a habit. When I was working out religiously before work doing P90X, I had to wake up at 6:30 a.m., six days a week. Was I good at this at first? No. Did I ever become a morning person? Absolutely not. But by doing it every day it did get a little easier, and in six months I had dramatic weight loss results. To be able to create a good habit, you must understand why you are doing it. I knew I wanted to lose weight, but why? To be healthier? *Check.* To feel better? *Check.* To look my best? *Check* … and many other reasons. Reaching your goal will require work and sacrifice. Dwayne "The Rock" Johnson (who I believe is in the best shape ever) is already in the gym by 4:00 a.m. to get a leg up over the "competition" (in his words).

It Will Never Happen

I know for a fact if you do nothing, you have failed 100 percent. Your dreams will never happen. They remain just that, dreams. I saw a T-shirt that said, "Die with memories, not dreams." Dying with a dream locked inside you, unrealized, is probably one of the saddest things that can

22 Andrew Merle, "This is When Successful People Wake Up" July 2017 https://www.huffpost.com/entry/this-is-when-successful-people-wake-up_b_596d17a3e4b0376db8b65a1a.

happen in life. There is always a good excuse, but never a good reason. And this happens every day. Maybe it is not written on tombstones or in obituaries or memorialized in eulogies or epitaphs, but you know when someone has lived a fulfilled life and when they have not.

What do you want your legacy to be? What do you want to be most remembered and revered for? I can tell you now they don't erect statues for the mediocre, the poor, or the average. They don't immortalize critics either. The people who are remembered the most are those who contributed to society, who really did amazing feats or succumbed to horrific tragedies. I hope that you are the former and not the latter.

When I look over the last twenty years of my life, I can see myself getting my undergraduate degree, moving to L.A., making multiple albums, videos, singles, getting my MBA, winning several awards, getting my DTM (Distinguished Toastmaster, the highest designation awarded, equivalent to an Eagle Scout in the Boy Scouts) from Toastmasters, starting several side businesses and ventures, and progressing in my corporate career. When I look toward the next twenty years, I see even more milestones, awards, and opportunities. What do you see in your past? Are you happy with the last twenty years of your life? What do you see in the future for yourself? Are you excited about the possibilities for the next twenty years of your life?

Even if you are not ecstatic about the last five, ten, twenty, years of your life, that doesn't mean you can't find a way to get more out of the next five, ten, or twenty years of your life. The question you need to ask yourself is, "What am I going to do with the rest of my life?" And how are you going to feel about it? Have you ever taken the time to ask yourself this?

In the legend of Socrates, as transcribed by Plato, the gods told Socrates that he was the wisest person alive at the time. He believed either everyone was ignorant, or he was the wisest because he knew his own ignorance and was quoted as saying, "What I do not know, I do not think I know." He was ascribed to "know thyself." Socrates concludes that "the unexamined life is not worth living." He believed his purpose was the search for truth. He accepted death as his fate, drinking the poison hemlock rather than live one day not fulfilling his purpose.

I do not think we have to go as far as Socrates, but I think in many ways that if we are living our life without a purpose, we are pretty much already dead anyway. Our dreams have died. Our hope has died. Our future is dead. But what was dead can be revived. And maybe it is not dead; maybe it's just dormant or sleeping.

In fact, the oldest mature seed that grew into a viable plant was a two-thousand-year-old date palm seed. It was excavated in Israel, subsequently planted, and germinated in 2005. I believe that the seed inside of you is still alive, can still be planted, grow, and spring up into a mighty tree, with the right environment and nurturing.

How Does Your Garden Grow?

As a kid, I learned the parable of the sower from the Bible. It is an allegory about a farmer who throws seeds indiscriminately, allowing them to be sown where they land at random. This parable is often referred to as the parable of the soils because it tells of four different types of soil situations that the seeds land in, and the outcome of their environment.

- The path or wayside (no soil)
- Rocky ground (little soil)
- Soil (with thorns)
- Good soil (fertile, with no issues)

In the first three scenarios, the seed is either taken away or fails to grow. In the fourth scenario, the seeds produce a full crop. Some of you today are struggling because your environment is not good. Your mindset is not good. Even if the dream or seed is good, it cannot grow in the environment or state you are in.

When I was stuck in a very pessimistic attitude, nothing went right. No one wanted to help me. No doors were opened. All I had to show for the time I toiled was strife and misery. When I changed my attitude and started "happening to life" instead of letting life happen to me, my luck turned around. When I had a negative attitude, I was putting that negativity out into the universe. I kept getting what I thought I would get: nothing. But once I started thinking, *Hey, I believe I can get what I want*, I started realizing those things in my life.

It did not happen overnight. You cannot plant a seed today and then expect the fruit to be ripe tomorrow. And if you did produce ripe fruit that quickly, I can guarantee it would not taste right or would be harmful to you. Good things take time. But you must plant today to reap tomorrow. That is a natural law that you cannot circumvent.

This is the secret to why some people or businesses can boom in bad times. During the most recent downturn in 2020 from COVID-19, I had planted so many seeds during the prior six to twelve months that all my hard work started to show results, even in the worst conditions. This was because I had set balls in motion that now were picking up momentum. What can you start planting today? What do you want to reap tomorrow?

The seed you plant is directly what you will reap. You cannot plant an apple tree and harvest bananas. That would be impossible. So if your dream is to write, and you start planting the seeds of writing a page a day, you could reap a book one year from now. If you start planting seeds to create music now, you will not be reaping a book in one year, unless it is a music book, and even then, you will still need to write it. Does that make sense?

Start Small

Who would have thought that an adopted college dropout who was tinkering around with computers in his parents' garage would eventually create one of the world's first trillion-dollar companies? This is exactly what Steve Jobs did with Apple in the 1970s. The same thing happened with Jeff Bezos at Amazon, and the founders of Google, Disney, Mattel, Box, Square, and Tesla. Nike was started out of Phil Knight's trunk, Dell out of Michael Dell's dorm room, the same with Mark Zuckerberg at Facebook. Black media entrepreneur Cathy Hughes built her radio empire, starting small with one fledgling AM radio station while homeless, living in her office with her young son.

If those companies had tried to start too big, too fast, the overhead and other issues would have killed them. To start, they employed a technique called "bootstrapping." Bootstrapping means a company starts small, with little to no money, and uses funds from initial sales to continually invest back into the business. Many businesses have been able to do this, and even a business of one can benefit from this technique as well.

Having nothing can be an advantage. Being unknown, if you fail, not many people will ever know. In the garage, there is safety. Necessity is also the mother of invention. When creating my record label, all I had was an idea but no money. Three years later, we have a little money, but now we are a full-fledged label, with online distribution, physical distribution, PR, radio promotion, and more. I wanted to create an outlet for myself, and eventually it created an outlet and opportunities for others.

If my venture had failed, I would have continued, but really it could not fail. I was already working on music and releasing it, so the label was an extension of that. Having nothing makes you resourceful. As Tupac said in "Dear Mama," his mom "made miracles every Thanksgiving." People who lived through the Great Depression learned how to live on turnip soup and straighten out bent nails to reuse them.

Coursehero blog explains how Dale Carnegie's landmark book *How to Win Friends and Influence People* came to be.[23] Originally, Dale set out just to give a small talk. Eventually that short talk became a ninety-minute lecture. The lecture eventually became a course, and the course needed a textbook. So he wrote some rules on a postcard, then a little bigger piece of paper, then a leaflet, then a series of booklets. After fifteen years, with multiple versions and changes, it finally became a full-length book that has sold over thirty million copies and was named one of *Time* magazine's one hundred most influential books.

I believe you should *dream* and *think big*, but you should always act and start small then grow *big* over time. There is a reason Napoleon Hill wrote *Think and Grow Rich.* Not *Go Big and Get Rich*. But most of us want instant instead of delayed gratification. We want the life hack. We want the biggest payoff as quickly as possible, but that is rare. Sometimes we plant trees whose shade we will never benefit from. Leonardo Da Vinci dreamed of a "flying machine" in 1498, but the Wright Brothers did not create a viable one until 1903, around four hundred years later.

23 https://www.coursehero.com/lit/How-to-Win-Friends-and-Influence-People/prefaces-summary/.

And the Wright Brothers made it without any government grants or deep pockets; they were just a couple of aviation enthusiasts. But they did not start out by building a plane. Their first invention was a small home-built wind tunnel, created to collect the most accurate data to help them design more efficient wings and propellers. While competitors started "big," making more powerful engines, the Wright Brothers focused on developing a reliable method for pilot control, creating the breakthrough three-axis control system, which enabled the pilot to steer the aircraft effectively and to maintain its equilibrium. This patented system remains standard on fixed wing aircrafts to this day! The problem with flying was not the engine, it was steering (direction) and equilibrium (balance).

Your problem, too, is your direction and balance. Where are you going? What are you focused on? Where you focus is where you steer. What parts of your life are out of balance? What is making you crash and burn? You will not soar with eagles if you hang around on the ground with turkeys!

Eric Ries popularized the term *minimum viable product*, or MVP, when discussing startups and entrepreneurs. It is a version of your product with just enough features to satisfy early customers who can test and provide feedback, but no more. Businesses are created to solve problems for the customers. You never want to assume you know what your customer wants; product developers tend to find that sample subjects are more forgiving and willing to provide useful feedback. Minimal cost is involved in building a functional prototype, and the feedback can help you ultimately create something better than what you might have originally. According to Ries, in an article on Medium.com entitled "Let's Focus on Validated Learning instead of Failing," he says the goal is to "*collect the maximum amount of learning with the least amount of effort.*" This saves you time and money. Also, you save on opportunity cost rather than paying a lot to go big only to bust (fail). Steve Blank sums it up by saying, "*You're selling the vision and delivering the minimum feature set to visionaries, not everyone.*"

Snowball Momentum

When I was a kid on the East Coast, I used to love snow days when school was cancelled; I'd go sledding and play in the snow. Imagine for a moment a freshly packed snowball, rolling down a snow-covered hill, picking up more snow and momentum, growing into a huge force to be reckoned with as it barrels toward the bottom. In psychology, this metaphor can be positive or negative. For this example, I am thinking about it as a positive force for good.

In the story of stone soup, two swindlers convince a group of townspeople that they can make soup from nothing. They then ask to borrow a pot, water, and eventually all the ingredients, and they end up making a soup big enough to feed the entire town. No one person had enough carrots, potatoes, or meat to make the soup on their own. It literally took a village to make it. You will pick up other people and other ingredients along the way—like the snow that your rolling snowball picks up.

When the snowball starts out, it may not be any bigger than your own fist, but it soon could be a huge ice boulder. Apple started as one computer. Netflix was just one DVD. Uber had just one car. Everything starts small before it grows big. Every mighty oak was once a lowly acorn. It takes one day to grow a mushroom and twenty years to make a mighty oak tree. Which do you want to be? How much time have you got?

Tony Robbins once said, "*Success comes from taking initiative and following up ... persisting. What simple action could you take today to produce a new momentum toward success in your life?*"[24]

KISS

When I think of KISS, I am not thinking of the makeup-wearing '70's rock band, nor a peck on the cheek from a loved one. I am thinking of the phrase "Keep It Simple, Son." This concept has helped me in many aspects of my life and career. We tend to overcomplicate the simple. Homemade chicken soup is a tried-and-true cure for almost all that ails you. And it has only a few ingredients: chicken, broth, veggies, sometimes noodles or rice, and seasoning.

Confucius said, "*Keep it simple and focus on what matters, don't let yourself be overwhelmed.*" What matters most to you?

24 Tim McLaughlin, "What Action Can You Take?" | Your Happiness Power" https://yourhappinesspower.com/what-action-can-you-take/.

You can have only so many top priorities in life. If everything is an emergency, how can you prioritise? To keep it simple, you must decide what the one thing is that matters most. If you could do only one thing for yourself today, what would it be?

I try to do one thing that will move the needle forward for me every day. That could be something that takes one minute or all day, but if that one thing gets done that day, I put that in the productivity "win" column.

Many people have told me I am very black-and-white in my approach to life, and they would be right. My friends say they admire my focus and dedication. What I do is not rocket science, and it is not something that only a chosen few can do. Anyone can manage to get simple tasks done daily. It just takes having a steel resolve.

Do you know what truly matters to you? What brings you joy? What makes you happy? I am quite sure you know what does not bring you joy or what makes you unhappy? So think about what the opposite is and do that instead. For example, I dislike raisins. I swap them out for dried cranberries in my trail mix. This is simple happiness. A life without raisins is just a little bit happier for me. What are your raisins? What can't you stand, and how can you fix that for yourself today?

What is the simplest solution? When I was learning how to cope with my anxiety disorder, taking pills seemed like the simplest solution, but it became complicated very quickly. I was told they could be highly addictive. Having a pill addiction made me feel anxious. So I decided not to take them and try natural remedies instead. I started meditating, praying, taking walks, going to therapy, and drinking herbal tea (reducing my caffeine). All simple remedies, all highly effective, and they had no side effects or addictive properties. Once you start looking for simpler, alternative solutions, the sooner you can start seeing incremental positive changes in your life, situation, or circumstance.

Answer These Questions:

1. What in the past has kept you from starting?
2. If you have started something, how do you track your progress?
3. If you have started something, how can you be faithful to complete it?
4. What project is on the back burner that needs to come to the front burner to get done?

5.

Goals Are Golden

> *"If you set goals and go after them with all the determination you can muster, your gifts will take you places that will amaze you."*
> — Les Brown, popular motivational speaker

In 2014, I became aware of TED Talks, an amazing series of events where thought leaders share ideas worth spreading. For example, Chris Pierce, a musician whom I know through my guitarist Luis Nariño, gave a TEDX talk about music and being deaf. It was great to hear such a vulnerable story coming from a musician I respect, admire, and happen to know. As I started getting into more TED Talks, hearing great speeches from Brene Brown, Simon Sinek, Reggie Watts, Sir Ken Robinson, and several more, Luis asked, "Why don't you do one, dude?"

I had never thought that I knew enough to speak about anything. I was not deaf. I love music and the arts, but I didn't think that would be engaging or interesting enough to add up to a talk. But like everything in life, I am often naive and believe everything can be researched and anyone can be contacted, so I started down a rabbit hole, figuring out how I could deliver a TED Talk. I started with my best friend, Google (because it knows everything about me, including all my secrets). I typed, "How do I give a TED Talk?" and in a few clicks I was on several blogs explaining how, eventually stumbling upon the TED website's list of contacts and dates for TEDX talks being given all around the world. I figured doing a TEDX talk would be much easier than getting on the official TED radar, but I was told that all the content would still be sent back to TED, the parent organization for these independent satellite, licensed speaking opportunities. I filled out about five applications for TEDX talks in California, then waited and eventually forgot about them. I was pleasantly surprised when I was emailed by TEDX Napa Valley about coming to perform. I immediately said yes and then called Luis, then my drummer, and my longtime friend from Berklee, Tony Hampton, to come perform with me.

Now that I had the gig booked, I started to dream about what I would say, what I would perform, and how I would make my moment on stage in front of four hundred people. As I kept watching more TEDX talks and performances, I quickly noticed that these people were professional and very polished. I did not want to get out there and make a fool of myself. I knew musically I would be fine, but this type of speaking in an auditorium would be different than my usual onstage banter, yelling in a crowded bar of drunk people looking to have a good time. This would be a captive audience looking to me to give them musical and intellectual gold. And that is when it dawned on me that I needed to make sure I had my "stuff" together.

In business school, I heard about Toastmasters International, a public-speaking and leadership nonprofit group that has helped thousands of people become better speakers over its ninety-plus-year existence. I did not have the time in school to join, as everyone said I spoke well, and I had no bandwidth to join anything else, but I had always kept it in the back of my mind. By 2014, I had been out of school for four years and missed the education system, so I thought I could check a lot of boxes by seeing what Toastmasters had to offer. I searched for a club in my town and found the Culver City Toastmasters Club, which meets every Tuesday evening in the Veteran's Memorial Building.

Starting anything new is both exciting and terrifying. Toastmasters can be very intimidating, even for someone like me who has spent a lot of his adult life on stage. It is different; it has a system and rules and protocols that take time to adjust to learn. But I quickly found that the group was very warm and friendly, and that it was comprised of a very diverse mix of people with the common goal to better themselves, learn leadership skills, and help others through service and mentorship.

It proved to not only be a great breeding ground to help sharpen my skills for my upcoming TEDX performance, but also for helping me with my humorous storytelling, for which I went on to win several awards in competitions, eventually leading to my earning the highest level of achievement in the organization, my Distinguished Toastmaster designation.

If You Aim For Nothing, You Will Hit It Every Time

The reason why I have been able to set out on new paths and achieve new desires is because I have learned and mastered the power of goal setting. Unfortunately, this is something that you will not learn in school. But goal setting can be learned, whether you teach it to yourself or ask for help from professional coaches or other resources. So many people I meet are not aiming for anything. If you do not take aim, then you are hoping and praying rather than planning and attacking.

Getting my MBA, doing a TEDx presentation, and completing Toastmasters all required goal setting. Once I set my sights on those goals, I made every plan and intention to finish that goal. If this is the first time you are thinking about making or setting a goal, then this might be difficult for you, especially if you are not naturally goal oriented. I have never heard of a scenario when someone setting a goal was not part of their success in achieving it. But I have heard countless stories of people who had no goal and who ended up with nothing.

I have heard Michael Jordan quoted as saying "You miss 100 percent of the shots you never take," which is definitely true, but at least in basketball you have the basket as a tangible, visible goal to aim toward. To win, you must sink the ball in the basket, and anyone can measure if you were successful or not. If you had no basket and just a ball and I said, "Toss it anywhere and see where it lands," you would say, "That's not basketball," and it wouldn't be the exciting game we watch on TV, the game that fills stadiums. A ball and no basket would make no sense. That would be a game called "stupid ball."

So the comparison is clear. Is it easier to see, then, how asinine it is to go through life without goals or without specific, well-planned, and executed goals? If you do not have goals, you are already losing. You have no way to measure how to win. If you are not trying to win, there is no point in playing the game. Just go sit down somewhere and be a spectator, because that is all you will be good for. Sit down and watch others succeed.

If that stings a little bit, then maybe that will light a fire under you to learn about goals and how to set them. You need to start learning what you do not know to improve your situation. Then, if you know what, but you don't know how, then there is still more that you need to know. But you are in luck. I am happy to offer five easy steps to help you start setting better goals.

Five Goal-Setting Steps:

1. Write down what you want to achieve.
2. Break down how you can achieve it.
3. Write down unknowns or connections you need to get there.
4. Do one thing each day to move the needle forward for yourself.
5. Stick to it, and if you miss a day, hop back on the next day.

Write Down What You Want To Achieve

For some of you, step one is going to be hard. Perhaps out of fear or not having all the facts lined up, some people will not be able to identify easily what they want. Sometimes I find it helpful to think about it in the negative. For instance, I can say I don't want to be poor. So I want to be ... rich. I don't want to be overweight, so I want to be ... fit. We are all aware of what we don't want out of life. And many of us do know what we want, but we have never had the courage or the aptitude to put it down on paper.

Putting your goals down on paper helps them become more real. You can see if they make sense or not. For instance, maybe I have a desire to become a professional basketball player, but there is no way I am going to write that down as a goal. I am not tall enough, and I lack the necessary motor skills. That's a fool's goal. Once the goal is written down, your kinetic memory helps you to hang on to it, and then you can start to break it down into smaller, quick bites.

Break Down How You Can Achieve It

Leave or create some space underneath the goal or goals you have written down to jot notes down on how you can achieve this. You need to note when you will check and how long it will take you to start and finish the goal. While I was writing this book, I created an outline and a writing/editing plan. I included the time of day, where I will write, software or tools, word count, and I even included a space for self-care—how I would take care of myself through the process. It helped to write this down before starting the process. I believe my organization of the process is one of the reasons why I succeeded this time around versus the other times I've tried; I had a better outline and plan. You can only eat an elephant a bite at a time. Breaking it down to the smallest common denominator and working your way back up to the bigger goal will make it seem that much more achievable. If you want to lose ten pounds in a month, thinking about it as two and a half pounds a week or 0.35 ounces a day seems much more manageable then trying to lose ten pounds all at once.

Write Down Any Unknowns Or Connections You Need To Reach Your Goal

There are no self-made people. Everyone needs someone to help. Just like the "Six Degrees of Kevin Bacon" game, any connection you need is just a few hops away. You can see the evidence for this by joining a platform like LinkedIn. So it's important to write down the things you don't know, like "I don't know how to self-publish" or "I need to find a literary agent." Writing down the connections and unknowns helps you see who you know, and who you need to know, and helps identify gaps in knowledge that you can fill through research or more connections over time.

Do One Thing Each Day To Move The Needle Forward For Yourself

I literally live this every day. I do just one thing that helps my career and personal aspirations along. I try not to overthink this. Whether it is sending an email to schedule a podcast interview, or writing a verse for a song, or recording a demo, or playing a show, or watching a webinar, or reading a book, or listening to music—I implement at least one thing that helps me on my way. It might take five minutes or all day, but it gets checked off and counts. But the one caveat is that the "one thing" must relate back to my smaller goals as well as to my overall goal. Otherwise, it does not count.

Stick To It, And If You Miss A Day, Hop Back On ASAP

Sticking to something, even if you don't feel like it, is the definition of perseverance or grit. If stick-to-itiveness were easy, we would see much richer, slimmer, happier people. It takes about eight years to become a doctor. If you make it only seven and don't finish, this ain't horseshoes and almost doesn't count. I have known people who went to medical school but didn't finish; they still have all the debt but no degree. That is a shame. I also know that for many, if they miss that first day of sticking to their goal, then they quit. From there, it can become a slippery slope of disappointing failures, one after another, making it harder and harder to hop back on the path. If you were in AA, for instance, and slipped and had a drink, your sponsor would help you to get back on the wagon immediately. If you take two steps forward and one step back, you will remain always one step ahead. But if you take two steps forward, then fall backward and stay there, you will never make it anywhere. Keep at it. You've got this! It is not about how you fail, but how you dust yourself off and try again. And the sooner the better.

Target Identified

It is easy to focus on your problems and obstacles, which can make it harder to see your target. The only way to make it to your destination is to never lose sight of it. In the Bible, when Peter walked on water out to Jesus, as long as he kept his eyes on the prize, he stayed afloat. But once he dropped his gaze and saw all the water around him, representing the problems in his life and the obstacles around him, he began to sink.

In long-range shooting, military-trained snipers are used to hitting a target six hundred meters away, with extreme long-range shooting being more than one thousand meters away. I have heard stories of a man who was able to use gear to shoot a target over three miles away. To be able to hit a target that far away, shooters are often paired with a spotter who uses gear to see where the bullet goes and to give suggestions according to the science of ballistics to adjust for wind and other factors. The easiest way to hit a target is for it to be both stationary and nearby.

To continue with this metaphor, you could never hit a target with your eyes closed. Vision is everything to make your dreams a reality. Most of us have some idea of what we want to do. But when we get busy, swept up in the affairs of the day, work, life, problems, obstacles, and issues, we lose sight of our vision, and our dreams often go by the wayside. Also, we do not take the necessary steps to be specific or exact. When playing darts, you earn points if your dart lands anywhere on the board, but the bullseye is the one worth the most points. You may get on the board in life, but if you don't hit the bullseye with laser focus, you will never be fully satisfied or fully reach your maximum potential. Remember, halfway to success is just "succ" (pronounced "suck"), and you don't want that, do you?

Philosopher Arthur Schopenhauer said, "Talent hits a target no one else can hit; genius hits a target that no one else can see." Being a good leader, or good businessperson, or good at what you do requires *talent*. Being a great leader, or great businessperson, or great at what you do requires *genius*. Seeing what no one else can see does not require a crystal ball, but it does require foresight, and often it requires a different vantage point or point of view.

In the military, a soldier sent ahead of the main force to gather intelligence on the enemy is called a "scout." The scout isn't necessarily any smarter than anyone else on the team, but he has the advantage of having more information because he can see things that the main force in the back has not. In the same way, you need to send a scout or be able to look ahead at what your competition is doing, and figure out how you can be a few steps ahead of them.

Once you have identified your target, you must then advance toward it, like a horse with blinders on. That way you will not be distracted. Lot's wife was told in the Bible not to look back, and when she did, she was gone, she was gone, turned to a pillar of salt. In life, you cannot go backward, only forward. If you want to reach your target as badly as you want to live and breathe, you will reach it. This is how people climb mountains, win Olympic medals, become captains of industry. A light can shine in the darkness, but a laser can cut through steel. You need laser-like precision and focus as you lock onto your target.

Don't give up. You will not hit your target if you stop or fall short. A job begun is only half-done. I have seen a lot of starters in my life, but I have seen far fewer finishers. Grant Cardone says, "Never drop your target; increase your actions." Jim Rohn exclaims, "Don't wish for it to be easier, wish for you to become better." That is the hard part. Everyone is sitting around wishing that life were easier. It is not that they do not have a target. It is that they have given up on reaching it because it is too hard. They say to themselves, "I wanted to be a dancer, but it was too physically demanding," or "I wanted to be a musician, but it was too competitive," or "I wanted to be a businessman, but I didn't have the money or connections." If that were true, how did some find the stamina, beat the competition, and get the money to succeed?

You can challenge your assumptions and beliefs at any time. People used to think the earth was flat, but now everyone knows that it is round. If you believe something is true, or you don't believe it is true, only thinking makes it so. Your mind will dictate what you focus on, and how you spend your time, money, and attention. Identify your target, and then let's get you the right weapon and skill to hit the bullseye.

Ready, Aim, Then Fire

What does it mean to get ready? If you tell a woodsman he has five minutes to chop down a tree—how would he do it? He would most likely spend the first two-and-a-half minutes sharpening his axe. Without the preparation, it would take more effort, strength, and possibly more time to chop down the tree. Rather, spending time preparing the axe ends up being more efficient. Could you do it being less prepared? Yes, but how many more trees could you cut down in half the time by preparing?

In the same way, after locking a target in sight, you must prepare to win.

How sharp is your axe right now? In his 1984 book *What They Don't Teach You at Harvard Business School*, author Mark H. McCormack tells a story attributed to Picasso in which Picasso is approached by a woman in a restaurant who sees him rapidly doodling on a napkin. She says,

"I would gladly pay whatever you think it is worth to have that," to which Picasso replies, "That'll be $10,000!" The woman is astonished and exclaims, "But you drew that in thirty seconds," to which Picasso retorts, "No, it has taken me forty years to do that!"

This story is a lesson on preparation as much as it is about knowing your worth. To be able to have more skill and speed takes education, practice, preparation time, and money. Whether this Picasso story is true or not, the idea is that the combination of all the years of hard work and preparation make the artist exceedingly valuable.

If you are upset that you are not worth more, I would ask what you have done the last ten, twenty, thirty, or forty years? Have you been constantly preparing and studying your craft like Picasso? Or have you been blowing in the wind, with no direction, hoping something will happen? I remember when I went home to play a series of shows in Maryland and my grandma came to see me. She remarked on how it had all seemed to come together. I had planned the show around a work trip, so I had work, visits with family and friends, and then performed two shows. I told her it did not just "come together" but was curated and planned specifically to work out the way it did.

The marksman who was able to hit that target three miles away said in an interview that he had to prepare and practice for weeks and weeks at a time, adjusting for wind, gravity, and many other factors to be able to make that shot. Because it is an exceedingly difficult, almost impossible shot to make, you can imagine his level of dedication and preparation.

How do you prepare? Do you even prepare? Have you ever used a recipe that states a certain amount of prep time and then a certain amount of cooking time? Some might skip prep, or prep as they go, but many would take the time to chop what needs to be chopped, preheat the oven or skillet, and so on; this process will aid in making whatever dish your heart desires. Why would you then not bring this mentality into your work or side hustle?

I find part of preparation to be fun. I do my best work in secret, toiling without judgment or criticism. In preparation mode, I am not trying to be perfect; I am just trying to understand what I need to get, to get to where I want to go. When I am working on a new piece of music or testing out new software, I really like to go deep and analyze all that can go wrong. I was prepping recently for a webinar I was giving about making vinyl records. I spent a whole weekend preparing slides and then going through my presentation. Upon starting the Zoom meeting, I tested my slides twice from Google slides, sharing from the app on my phone and had no issue; but I had received a call and it kicked me out of Zoom. Upon returning, the webinar was starting, so I had to prepare to begin. When the host turned it over to me, I went to share my slides, and lo and behold, like Murphy's Law, it did not work. Luckily, I have spent years in Toastmasters learning how to stay calm in a presentation and how to speak off the cuff, and I was able to deliver the twenty-minute presentation without my slides (luckily it was a talk about myself, something I know quite a lot about).

In Toastmasters, we often say you must always be prepared to be prepared. In fact, as civil rights leader Whitney M. Young put it: "*It is better to be prepared for an opportunity and not have one than to have an opportunity and not be prepared.*" I always, in my mind, rehearse my speech ahead of time so that I know my talking points, anticipating that technology from time to time will fail. I heard of a speaker who ended up giving a talk in complete darkness due to a power outage; he was still able to speak, even if he could not see the audience. In a way, it allowed him to paint better word pictures to make up for the lack of gestures and props, while also using vocal variety, metaphors, and other skills.

If you start without planning and preparation, you will hit many pitfalls along the way that could have been prevented or mitigated by taking time to think them through. Einstein believed in having thought experiments, that is, thinking through scenarios before ever actually attempting anything on paper or in the laboratory. In the same way, you can think about the best way to achieve your goal and the best plan of action. Before starting your course, you should be charting your course.

One of my media heroes, billionaire mogul Oprah Winfrey, believes that "luck is preparation meeting opportunity. If you hadn't been prepared when the opportunity came along, you wouldn't have been lucky." So any of you thinking right now that you need a little bit of luck, or feel like you have been unlucky in life, you really have not been unlucky—simply unprepared.

Locked And Loaded

I am happiest when I am productive, so I try to minimize time doing nothing. The term *locked and loaded* comes from a military phrase that means your weapon has been locked for safety (so you don't shoot by mistake) and loaded (you have loaded ammunition into the gun's chamber). Your ammunition is your purpose and your passion. This is your potential. Potential is stored-up energy, ready to be used when needed so you don't go off half-cocked, shooting willy-nilly. A lot of terms used in this chapter come from the military because a lot of great business and strategic analogies and quotes come from war.

The war we are fighting most of all right now is the war within ourselves. The battle between what we know we should be doing and what we are doing. We are competing against conflicting messages, outdated beliefs, and the myriad of distractions jockeying for our time, energy, minds, and bodies. In *The Art of War*, author Sun Tzu says, "*One may know how to conquer without being able to do it.*" In our heads we may know, I should be doing x, but the crux of this book is to show *how* you can do x while also maintaining y. Y being your main gig; x being what you ultimately want to do or what you enjoy doing the most that fulfills your purpose.

My sweet spot in life is figuring out how to allot time and allocate resources to what I want to do. This did not come easily. I have had periods in my life when I have done more or less what I wanted to do, but in the end, I always did *some* of what I wanted to do. When I know my day job is going to be busy, I plan and adjust accordingly. We all can benefit from foresight, understanding, and planning for what is to come. If you know you have a huge deadline at work, then you may have to allocate almost all your time to it and put some of your "play" onto the back burner. But when work ebbs and flows and you have more time, you can move that "play" back to the front burner.

What should you load into your arsenal to be ready? As we have discussed, for many of you, you will need a website, an online portfolio or proof of concept to be able to show people. For others, you may need to create content, marketing, audio/visuals, and other tools to help people understand what it is that you do. Since a lot of this book has to do with self-help, I have been reviewing techniques with a group of mentees for free in a bi-weekly call, in the hopes of helping them move towards their purpose. I am doing that to be a good friend and to give back, but I am also doing it to prove that the ideas presented here do work. People may not have time to read a book, but they always have time to learn from the pages of someone else's life experience. Your knowledge, your expertise, and your work experience can be invaluable to someone else who wants to be where you are. I believe everyone could write a book about something they know about. And if you cannot today, then I would suggest loading into your arsenal all the books, podcasts, webinars, online courses, and whatever other educational content you can get your hands on.

You must lock in that knowledge so it does not escape. Our brains are often overloaded with information, and we forget a lot of what we see, hear, and read. Most knowledge won't stick. Even if you only remember some of what you see, hear, and read, it's important to lock and load the things you do recall, those things that can serve you on your journey today. Even small percentages of retention are plenty to keep in your arsenal for now.

What is one thing you've learned recently that made you say to yourself, "Man, I wish I had known this sooner." I recently started taking a real estate course; I am learning that cash flow and passive income are part of the path to wealth. When I was younger, I spent so much time just trying to survive, I didn't think about learning how to really become wealthy. I knew there were things that I didn't know, but I didn't know what they were. I remember being at my ex-girlfriend's place, flipping through channels, and landing on CNBC and the Suze Orman show. She was the first person to break down for me that people with consumer debt and other obligations might not have as much money as they thought they did. Not everything she said I agreed with, but I did like watching her show and reading her books and column in *O, The Oprah Magazine*. I thought to myself, *Man, If I had known this information earlier, I would have done a lot of things differently. But I know it now, and I need to be thinking about what to do with this newfound knowledge.*

A soldier who is locked and loaded may never have the chance to use their gun, but they would not want to be caught by the enemy unarmed.

This is what happens every time an opportunity arises that we are not prepared for. We are caught like a deer in headlights, frozen. Sun Tzu also taught to "*attack [your enemy] where he is unprepared, appear where you are not expected.*" This is what good competitors do to business competition every day. You must always be prepared and expect the unexpected. You make a rainy-day fund because you know one day it is going to rain, and, unlike Noah, unless you have prepared an ark, your whole existence could wash away right before your eyes.

Forget about all the things you didn't know; instead, take what you do know now and start building the biggest war chest you can create. In a great war chest there are maps, weapons, ammunition, strategy papers, and other tools and artefacts that could help you to win the battle raging all around you and win in life.

Make Sure The Ladder You Are Climbing Is On The Right Building

All my life I have heard the phrase, "Climb the corporate ladder." The notion of climbing a metaphorical ladder, rung by rung to success, started in the nineteenth century, but it was not until the twentieth century when Allen Raine added a cautionary refrain: "You may get to the very top of the ladder, and then find it has not been leaning against the right wall." How often have we gotten everything we wanted, only realizing after it was not actually what we wanted at all? You must be careful when reaching and climbing toward your purpose and destiny that you are constantly checking that the ladder is leaning against the right building.

I have seen many businesses pivot only to eventually become something that they did not recognize. I am sure Enron didn't set out to defraud people. When I was younger, I wanted to study to become a doctor, but I quickly realized that that was my aunt's dream (she became a chemist) and not my own. Once I realized this, I sunk all my energy into my true passion of making music.

Any dream you want to make come true must be *your* dream. We are most passionate about what fulfills us most; you can lie to everyone, but not to yourself. If your heart's not in it, it will be almost impossible to make it happen. That does not mean we cannot from time to time help others with their dreams. I actually think we should do that, to be a good friend, and just to be a helpful neighbor in life. But it also helps to create a decision tree that includes asking the questions. Is this my dream? Does this action move me closer to or farther from my dream? Is it benign or neutral (that is, neither moves me forward or backward from my dream?)

"Is this the right goal for me, right now, at this point in my life and career?" This is a question I often ask myself. I am aware that my goals will change based on bandwidth and other life changes. And that is okay. Goals are not set in stone; they should be constantly reevaluated and adjusted. Sometimes you are climbing a ladder that is leaning against one building, but you need to come down the ladder and move it to a new building, then start your climb again. The beauty of this is you have learned so much by climbing the previous rungs that you can use that skill in climbing the rungs in front of you now.

Life's Teachable Moments

For those who believe in reincarnation, this provides an opportunity for the soul to learn one new thing after another or to keep at one thing until you've mastered it. I believe that in every circumstance, a lesson is wrapped inside, a nugget of truth to mine, especially from our failures. Failure is nothing more than an experiment with a false hypothesis. But it is also the opportunity to make a change and create a new hypothesis, one that might prove true.

When I was taking the Financial Peace University course with Dave Ramsey, he would explain how, as a parent, he would offer his kids teachable moments about money—teaching them to give, save, and spend with the small wages that they earned by working and doing chores. He also taught them how to be a contributing member of the family (no allowance paid for that), and to be able to think about delayed gratification and working and saving up for things they wanted.

My parents taught me many things, but they also left me with huge gaps in knowledge that I have been trying to fill my entire adulthood. And now they sometimes come to me for advice, rather than vice versa. Their parents could not teach them; therefore they could not teach me. I taught myself about personal finance, buying stock, and several other financial principles to set myself up for success. I have always seen the value of learning, even from a young age.

If there is something you need to learn, what is keeping you from doing so? There are so many affordable or free classes about a variety of subjects; almost any type of "how-to" content exists on blogs or YouTube. The public library is still free and open to the public. There is no excuse not to learn. Albert Einstein believed that "*intellectual growth should commence at birth and cease only at death*." That means that the dash in between your birth and death on your tombstone indicates when you lived and the time you had an opportunity to learn.

In the Bible, young Solomon was told he could ask God for one gift. He could have asked for money, fame, longer life, or whatever he could imagine, and he decided wisely to ask for wisdom. With wisdom, all things are possible. He became the wisest man who ever lived, he was able to amass wealth and fame, and I venture he had wisdom about how to live that afforded him better health and longevity as well.

You will see that I did not state anything about formal education here, as I know that not everyone will learn in school or university.

Start to make a priority list of things you need to learn and ways to attain that knowledge today. There is no point to focus on trying to figure out what you don't know you don't know. Just start with what you already know you don't know, and that will be plenty. Again, we already mentioned earlier how much we end up forgetting, so know that in this journey of lifelong learning, you will have to continue to put new thoughts and ideas into your arsenal over time. What you have forgotten or don't know could make a whole other world!, but what you know and can learn in this lifetime is more than enough to start.

Plan Before You Build; Call Before You Dig

A friend of mine from college told me her dad made millions coining the idea of "call before you dig" at construction sites. This meant contacting the city planning offices to get specifics on a dig site to avoid causing structural damage to the properties or hitting pipes or subterranean obstacles that contractors and developers may not know about.

Earlier, I mentioned SCORE, a group of volunteer mentors who help budding entrepreneurs avoid pitfalls. You can learn with someone who has dug where you are about to dig and can let you know certain traps to avoid. SCORE services are free. The SBA also lists a lot of free or discounted resources.

In the music business, when creating an album, there is a part of the process called preproduction, which I have found to be especially important to cost and time savings. Preproduction involves gathering your song list, checking you have your song forms down, understanding structure, instrumentation, which players you want to hire and other personnel (engineers, producers), documenting your songs in writing (charts, sheet music, scores, lyric sheets), determining BPM (beats per minute), keys, and possibly demoing the songs before recording fully. Other arts like film, TV, commercials, and music videos all have a preproduction phase. This is when you would also figure out your budget.

In the Bible there is a parable in Luke that explains about understanding the cost:

> *"Suppose one of you wants to build a tower. Won't you sit down and estimate the cost to see if you have enough money to complete it? For if you lay the foundation and are unable to finish it, everyone who sees it will ridicule you, saying, 'This person began to build and wasn't able to finish'"* (Luke 24:28–30).[25]

That person would be perceived as foolish. If you think that what you are trying to accomplish won't cost you something, it could end up costing you everything.

Zig Ziglar stated that after his first baby, he did not have enough money to get her out of the hospital or to pay the bill for her delivery. He said, paraphrased: "I was a great salesman. I sold my house, I sold my car, I sold everything that wasn't practically nailed down." Everything in life has a cost, and it is up to you to understand what that is and if you are willing to make the sacrifice to pay for it and continue paying for it.

On the game show *Who Wants to Be a Millionaire?* there used to be a feature called "phone-a-friend." This allowed the contestant to call

25 Luke 14:29, "NIV – For if you lay the foundation and are [...]" https://www.biblegateway.com/passage/?search=Luke+14%3A29&version=NIV.

someone they knew who they thought was an expert on the subject to give them advice. Who would be your phone-a-friend? Who has the information you most desperately need to get ahead? And how can you gain access to them? I spent considerable time going through a MasterClass online about jazz taught by Herbie Hancock, which came with a lifetime membership for eighty-five dollars to view his twenty-five-plus video content, plus a course textbook. I would never be able to afford to take private lessons with him but was able to gain the benefit and knowledge as if I had for much less. Where there is a will, there is a way. You can gain knowledge and access to any subject and person you can think of, or a reasonable substitute, that can get you further up the road. Do your due diligence. Seek out the people and the knowledge that you need.

I knew someone who was working on a multifamily commercial property renovation where the contractor did not survey the site properly. A major pipe burst, leaving the residents without hot water for weeks and costing the company millions of dollars in damage, hotel costs, rental credits, and several other issues. Not checking before you start working can be an awfully expensive, costly mistake. Find out who you need to call first and make that call. It will save you time, money, and headaches, trust me.

SMART Goals Only

Working in the corporate world, the idea of creating SMART goals comes up often. It is a particularly important tool, just like SWOT (strength, weakness, opportunity, threat) Analysis and a variety of other business tools I have used over the years. For those of you who may not yet be familiar, I suggest learning the basics, as it helps you in your goal setting. It essentially helps you create better, more defined goals by making sure they are Specific, Measurable, Achievable, Relevant, and Time Bound. The idea comes from a 2003 book by Paul J. Meyer, *Attitude Is Everything: If You Want to Succeed Above and Beyond.* I will briefly outline how you can use these in your work/life.

Specific: What do you want to do? Why do you want to do it? Who is needed? Where will you do it? What resources are involved? What constraints exist?

Example: Instead of saying I want to excel in my career, say I want to become a C-level executive in my company. This way we know exactly what you want, whereas the first statement is ambiguous about how you would know you achieved that goal.

Measurable: This is how you will create metrics or key performance indicators (KPIS) to know if you have achieved your goal or not. If you wanted to train to run a marathon, you would need to be able to run 26.219 miles. So, once you were able to run that far, you would know you have trained enough to be able to complete one marathon. Then you can measure accurately if the goal was met or not.

Achievable: Your goal must be realistic. You can have a stretch goal, but it cannot be completely out of reach. If you wanted to go back to school and get your master's degree, the fastest you could probably do it is twelve months. You could not then set a goal that you would like to earn a master's degree by next month. No matter how hard you tried, that goal would not be attainable.

Relevant: Is this really what I want to do? Is this the time to work toward it? Is my current environment conducive for this goal? If you made a goal to start a career but also have the goal to start a family, and starting a family is more important to you, it might not be as relevant to climb the corporate ladder, knowing that you may not be able to continue based on needing to leave that job for an extended period of time. It might mean you want to start your family first, and then a few years later re-enter the workforce and start your climb when the environment and your personal situation is more conducive. That is not to say you cannot do both at the same time; it would just be harder and would require some extra steps, and you might feel pulled into opposite directions at once.

Time Bound: How long will this take? When will I achieve that? You will have short- and long-term goals. Some you can do daily, some will take weeks, some months, some years. But you cannot just say, "I would like to release an album." You need to say,

"I would like to release an album in the next twelve months." This creates a ticking clock that can keep you on task and that you can use to break down your larger goal into bite-size chunks, such as three months to write songs, three months to record, three months to create artwork, and three months to create marketing plans and set up for your release. If you get to a year from now, you know if you achieved this in time or not. If you say, "Someday I will get this done," that day may never come.

You Must Have Independent Goals

Don't pick a goal that is entirely reliant on external forces you can't control. I cannot make a goal that says "I will win a Grammy next year," because that relies on votes from Academy members that I may never get. But I can say I would like to submit a project to be considered for a Grammy, as I am a voting member, have access to the platform, and am eligible to do it 100 percent on my own.

Other Considerations

Some feel that SMART goals can lack flexibility or creativity. But remember, this is only a mnemonic device to help you better set goals, but it is not the only path. All goals need to be continually reevaluated. As you gain more information, you may find your goal is not attainable, or you really do not want it after all, or a priority in your life has shifted so you have to realign your goals or reprioritize them. I do not believe these need to be carved in stone, but they do need to be documented, allowing for changes as needed.

As Bill Copeland once said, "The trouble with not having a goal is that you can spend your life running up and down the field and never score."[26] In this scenario, all you will end up doing is frustrating and tiring yourself. I do not believe making a SMART goal will have an adverse effect on your outcome, but I believe that not having a goal that is

26 "How to Manage Your Money Like a CEO – EndThrive" https://endthrive.com/rules-of-money/.

properly defined with a clear focus and scope will make it almost impossible to achieve it.

If you are reading this book, you are looking for an answer to the problem of how you can achieve what you want to achieve. Many of you have wasted a lot of years not doing that. It is not about doing this 100 percent right. You will make many, many mistakes, often along the way, but you will fall and get back up again. You will learn something you didn't know before. You will push yourself to new limits and heights. Picasso believed that *"Our goals can only be reached through a vehicle of a plan ... there is no other route to success."*

The adage is true that if you fail to plan, then you are planning to fail. Not having a goal is like hopping in the car with no destination and no map, so when you end up nowhere, wasting time, money, and gas, why would you think it would end up any different? Many of us have been working so hard to merely survive that we have not set goals to move beyond that to self-actualize.

Answer These Questions:

1. How can you break down your dreams into goals?
2. What baby step goals can you start making daily?
3. Are you wishing and hoping, or are you planning and taking action?

6.

Don't Just Survive, Learn To Thrive

> *"My mission in life is not merely to survive, but to thrive; and to do so with some passion, some compassion, some humor and some style."* —Maya Angelou, poet

I, like many Americans, emerged from undergrad and grad school with an alarming six-figure debt. Higher education is essentially mortgaging our future. Sure, in the long term, those with degrees usually fare better than their non-degree-holding counterparts, but in some ways their non-degree friends are better off. I heard one person say you are richer at six years old than at twenty-two, because at six you are in the black and at twenty-two you are deeply in the red. School and the diploma/degree don't mean very much; the only thing school taught me was how to learn and to think for myself. We have a lot of forces working against us when coming out of school. The days of having a degree and getting a job because of that degree are gone. Maybe thirty to forty years ago that was the case, but by now so many people have degrees that the applicant pool has more applicants than job openings. Almost all jobs require experience, experience you can only get on the job. So, it's a catch-22. Pair that with being in the middle of a recession, with a hyper unemployment rate, as once happened to me. I spent five months looking for a job, found one, was let go in three months, and then spent another five months looking for work. I quickly went through my savings, was ineligible for unemployment, and thus used credit to finance everything until it was maxed out, and then I stopped paying everything.

This was probably one of the most painful experiences I ever went through at age twenty-seven in 2010. I had never been sued before; all three of my credit cards sued me that year for failure to pay. I would get so many calls from collectors, I stopped answering my phone until my phone was shut off for failure to pay. Then my car had an issue, and I could not afford to get it fixed, and the bank was emailing me that they would need to repossess it, to which I never replied. (It was not parked at my residence, so they did not find it, luckily.) My family either did not have the funds or did not want to help me (they sent their free prayers, maybe they helped), and, really, it was not their responsibility. I had to learn to clean up my own financial mess. I had to sublet my apartment to my best friend and sleep on her couch while I figured out how to recover from rock bottom.

The beauty of hitting rock bottom is that there's nowhere to go but up. When losing a lot of money, many will liken it to experiencing a death. You go through all the stages of grief, and in many ways I did die. The old me was dead. I had to walk in a brand-new me. But when there is a crisis, there is also an opportunity. I knew halfway through business school that the information about finance I was learning was great for a corporation valuation but was not going to help me balance my checkbook. I had already started listening to Suze Orman and, later, Dave Ramsey. Having knowledge did not help my income problem, but I knew that eventually I would find a job, and whatever job it was, I would try my hardest to pick up the broken pieces of my financial life, through all the missteps, false starts, and failures, and start to make better decisions with money.

I finally landed a new job in e-commerce for a beauty company, in which I ended up progressing, staying for almost eight years. The secret to this successful turnaround started when I decided to take the bull by the horns and steer it in the direction I wanted it to go, instead of it pushing me around. I started thinking about ways that I could stop surviving and start thriving, and these are three of the principles and lessons I learned through that experience: broke is not poor, you have been through worse, and delayed gratification is your friend.

Broke Is Not Poor

Being broke is temporary; poor is forever. Being poor is a mentality, and a bad one to have. Unfortunately, many will never escape poverty.

While I empathize, I also know that many could escape it if they changed their habits and allowed for paradigm shifts. As an adult, I had to change my assumptions and beliefs, as they were often wrong. For example, as a kid, my entire family (all female) was deathly afraid of cats. Why? I have no idea. Growing up, we would see a cat and instantly all of them would go into fight-or-flight mode and hop up on tables as if they had seen a rat. I made it a point growing up to force myself to be around cats so I would not grow up fearing them for no apparent reason. I have lived with cats. I have held cats, fed cats, and slept next to cats. I have no issues with them.

My point is this: it would have been very easy for me to just be afraid of cats because my mom, aunts, grandma, and great grandma were all afraid of cats. But as I thought about my interaction with cats, I had not been bitten by a cat, or scratched. I never had any bad interactions or saw anything in a scary movie that would have scarred me for life being around cats.

The same principle applies with money. How you think about money affects how you interact with it. If you grew up with the feeling of not having enough, where no one ever talked about money except to say there wasn't any, you can choose to have a different association and experience with money. Bob Proctor said in a recent webinar, "Money comes where it is invited." When you speak negatively about money, you are inadvertently uninviting it into your home. I remember all the times I learned to save money on my own as a kid, from rolling pennies at age six to buying Mother's Day gifts for my family, to getting my first job at McDonald's and saving my first thousand dollars in a new savings account, all in one summer. During my personal financial low, the power to save was still inside me but had been dormant. It had to be reactivated.

You Have Been Through Worse

When you lose everything, you think it is the end of the world. But as you zoom out of your life, no matter how bad it is, it sucks the worst when you are living it. As I think about these events ten years later, they cause me absolutely no pain. Sure, I have the scars, I remember what it felt like, the same way I remember splitting my hand open at nine years old. But like that scar, it is only a reminder. I do not open up the wound daily to revisit it. I had other childhood traumas that were much worse—all kinds of abuse I suffered and lived through. And though it took a lot of therapy to work through that, and it took me time to make it through the financial setback, I made it and was better for it on the other side. What did Winston Churchill say? *"If you're going through hell, keep going."*

I used to write my mom emails about all the growing pains I was going through in my early twenties, and a few years ago I ran across some of them, and they were funny. As I saw my younger self baring my soul to my one true confidante. I realized that all the problems I had back then had dried up. There was not one problem from yesterday that was affecting me today, yet I know I will face new problems tomorrow. Don't worry so much about what you are going through now; just know that where you start is not where you will end.

Delayed Gratification Is Your Friend

To be able to save and to sacrifice means believing in delayed versus instant gratification. There is a hilarious experiment called the "Marshmallow Test," in which an adult gives one child a choice: they can have one marshmallow that is sitting on the table in front of them now, or they can have another marshmallow (that's two) in five minutes (which is an eternity to a six-year-old), if they do not touch the first marshmallow during that time period. Then they proceed to leave the child alone in the room and videotape their reactions. I don't know if this is supposed to be funny, but you see many kids look intensely at it, sigh, huff and puff, and touch it ever so gently. One kid just eats it immediately. (Who hasn't been there?) A rare few wait the entire time and get the second marshmallow, but most do not.

It's funny seeing the delayed gratification experiment with children, but as adults we are not much better. Many of us can't wait to spend all the money we have, or waste all our time doing everything but what would fulfill our purpose. It is a very hedonistic approach to life. Those people usually end up in lots of debt, have addiction issues, and a myriad of other problems. Everyone who is successful has learned some degree of delayed gratification—they are delaying spending money or spending time doing things that are more fun to be able to invest in their future.

Get To The Top Of The Pyramid

To get to the top stage of self-actualization, as described in Maslow's Hierarchy of Needs, you first have four other levels of basic and psychological needs you must get through. This is why many of us merely survive and never really thrive. In fact, if a baby does not hit certain marks at checkups, the medical term for it is called "failure to thrive." Some of us are little runts who never had the opportunity or resources to have all our needs met to be able to succeed. That is why Darwin talks about survival of the fittest. His theory has to do with pure genes and does not account for medical and scientific breakthroughs, and it does not say that person lived up to their potential, only that they lived.

Psychologist Abraham Maslow discovered that people want to self-actualize, achieve their full potential, including creative pursuits, if they could have all their other needs met. He developed these theories while trying to understand and explain human motivation—why we do the things we do (or don't do). The theory of being able to ascend is fascinating; some would even say I have an obsession about it, which I believe is a good thing. I wanted to know how I could reach the top. In Zig Ziglar's motivational books, *See You at the Top* and *Over the Top*, he said that the bottom is mediocrity. If you want to be average, there is no point in trying to learn anything or set goals. In my mind, you have to aim for the top to be the best. There is no substitute for self-actualization. You either live up to your full potential or you don't.

You have to be careful, though. You don't want to climb to the top and either be standing on a bunch of skeletons or look around and have no one to share it with. That is why the other levels of needs (Physiological, Safety, Belonging/Love, and Esteem) are important to obtain first. The poverty line in America is around $10,000 for a single person and $22,000 for a family of four annually. This does not take into consideration the cost of living in every area, and would be the minimum standard to be able to eat daily, not including housing, etc. At current market value, you would need food stamps and Section 8 subsidies just to survive. Another study concluded that an individual would need to make $75,000 to be happy. Now they are saying there is no real number—you could be happy at any level as a choice, but I think $75,000 is the truer poverty line for an individual.

What does this mean? It means that you would need a certain amount of money to have all your needs met to begin to save and invest for the future and to self-actualize. So, to all those people who say money can't buy you happiness, they are half right. Money has no feelings; it is just a tool, and the love of it could very well be foolhardy. But there is a minimum amount needed to survive and later thrive. This is never properly explained in school. So, what does this mean for you? It means if you are not realizing your full potential, if you are working but are constantly tired and not getting anywhere, you are what is defined as the "working poor." But again, that definition of falling under the poverty line, whether it be spending a considerable amount of time looking for work while unemployed, the poverty line as currently defined is inaccurate. The numbers for the poverty rate are about 12 to 14 percent, and the working poor is about between 1 and 19 percent.

There are two conflicting schools of thought on how to help one get out of poverty: one believes the government should provide more welfare and assistance (give a man a fish); the other feels we should help individuals become more self-sufficient (teach a man to fish). I think we probably need a mixture of both. It would be hard to teach a man to fish when he is hungry, but it would be unsustainable to continually keep giving him a fish when he is able to catch his own; and he will feel better about himself doing what he can on his own (self-esteem).

A man whose belly is full and is no longer in danger of going hungry again with the knowledge of knowing how to fish for himself, with plenty of fish in the sea, is now ready to take time for self-reflection, to think, and begin to self-actualize.

Maslow has been criticized in recent years as he, like many who study success, chose to study the top 1 percent of performers, not the other 99 percent. His methodologies may be problematic, but we can clearly see his studies have crossed over from science to psychology and sociology. I personally have no issue with studying the best of the best. If you want to be the best, who better to model and pattern yourself after?

I feel we are a product of nurture and our environment. What we see drastically affects us. Bob Proctor says that the subconscious mind is just a sponge, unlike the conscious mind, which can reason and accept or deny things put into it; therefore, subconsciously it can only accept data, it cannot refute. The Apostle Paul wrote, "*Whatever is true, whatever is noble, whatever is right, whatever is lovely, whatever is admirable—if anything is excellent or praiseworthy—think about such things.*" (Philippians 4:8). Self-actualization begins and ends with the mind and mindset.

Don't Be A Dodo

Dodos have unfortunately become a footnote in the annals of history as a warning to not become extinct or obsolete. They were known to be stupid and easy to catch. Some might attribute this to fearlessness rather than stupidity, and nothing lasts forever, but once you stop evolving, you start to die out. We as a species have the choice to evolve or not. Man has existed for thousands of years, and we have had multiple evolutions and revolutions; in fact, the written word is part of us evolving. Before the written word, we passed down stories orally, and before that we drew our stories on cave walls.

I want to leave more than a footnote behind. I want to leave a footprint in cement, not sand. Why did the dodo die out and not the chicken, turkey, penguin, or ostrich? They are all flightless birds and yet they are still here, while the hapless dodo is no more. What can we learn from them?

I have heard it said that humans use about 10 percent of their brain. Our knowledge and capacity for growth is limited only by our foresight, aptitude, and imagination. There are several simple ways for you to boost your brain power:

Believe You Are: There is a lot we do not understand about the mind, but one thing we do know is that it believes what we say is true, whether it is true or not. This means that you can start thinking and believing you are smarter, and you will be. I recently listened to a Brian Tracy audio program on confidence. He told a story of a businessman needing to turn his business around who had had a chance meeting with John D. Rockefeller, who gave him a check for $500,000. The man placed the check for safe keeping in the safe in his office and started conducting business better, knowing he had a check in the bank he could cash at any time, from one of the richest men in America. The man was told to come back in one year, after having a year of sales, and pay Rockefeller back by check. When the businessman returned to the same spot one year later, he saw the old man emerge from the shadows once again, but this time a nurse was following quickly behind him. The nurse said to the businessman, "Sorry. I hope this old man has not been any trouble. He escapes from this nursing home often and has a fascination with telling people he is John D. Rockefeller!" The old man and the check ended up being fake, but the businessman's belief in both made him conduct business more confidently, and his results were real too!

The point of the story is you do not need to meet the richest man in the world and receive riches to be able to start living and walking in the life you want. All you need to do is start believing you *can* have those things. I know to some it sounds too good to be true—if everyone believed this, everyone would be rich, skinny, etc. But it is a good start. If you believe you are smarter and start making smarter decisions, smarter choices, reading smarter books, and doing other things to improve yourself, you will see a difference in your life.

Health Is Wealth

Attending to your health is important too. Getting proper rest at night and taking naps has been found to improve brain function. The body repairs itself during sleep, including brain cells, by powering down our conscious brain. I have always had trouble sleeping eight hours, but I love taking naps as needed. In Spain, they take a *siesta*, a two-hour break after lunch, and show remarkable productivity afterward. I have never understood why the siesta did not come over to America. We rush eating our lunch, or barely get out into the sunshine. Americans are notorious for being less happy at work than other countries, as evidenced by all the indigestion, ulcers, GERD, and other issues.

Exercise is also a great way to improve circulation and brain activity. A healthy body and a healthy mind go hand in hand. There are many studies that show a direct link between people who have suffered mental trauma who have had a myriad of physical health manifestations, including anxiety, depression, strokes, and heart attacks. Exercise releases endorphins and serotonin in the brain, which helps people feel better, both physically and emotionally.

Social activity also makes you smarter. Staying connected even during times where distance keeps us apart is important. Now there are so many online tools, like Zoom and social media, that allow us to keep in touch. The need for human contact has been well documented. In fact, abandoned babies need to be held and touched for personal development. Essentially, if you leave a baby unattended, but feed it and give it water but never hold it, it can easily develop an intellectual disability. It has to do with lacking certain stimuli in its formative years that teaches it essentially that the stimuli it is looking for is not coming. In response, certain parts of the baby's brain don't develop normally. It is imperative to stay socially active, even for those extreme introverts, and find a way to connect comfortably, even from the comfort of your own home.

Smarter With Age

As we age, our intelligence changes. An article by *Business Insider* says we get wiser and smarter with age. Some skills peak in our teens, like fluid intelligence, the ability to think quickly and recall information (think senior moments), but other abilities "like reading others" emotions, to recalling events, peaks at 30, and our ability to do basic math and use large vocabulary, peaks at 50. At any age, you still have a lot of life and mind left. Your brain is the best, fastest, smartest supercomputer you will ever own.

Challenging yourself, taking classes, doing puzzles, and reading books—all these things help to increase intelligence. Even if you may never get invited into Mensa, it doesn't mean that you cannot learn and grow your entire life.

What's The Difference?

To thrive or not to thrive? That is the question. What is the major difference between thriving and surviving? When I was a kid, we did not always have money for eating out, and so I quickly learned that sometimes I would have to eat things that I didn't want (to survive) instead of being able to go out and eat (thriving). In the long run it was probably better eating those home-cooked meals rather than fast food or restaurant fare, but the realization that we did not have an endless supply of money stuck with me. I wanted to grow up and be able to eat out when I wanted to; luckily, I am now fortunate to be able to do so.

It really is that simple. The major difference is that those who thrive can call their own shots. They have risen to a level where they have amassed wealth and have the luxury of their time being their own. The people who wake up angry, "having" to work instead of "wanting" to work, are the ones stuck in survival mode and, as you can tell, it is often unpleasant. Many of those people not only "have to work" but "have to work" a job they hate, doing rudimentary things that are unfulfilling, and dealing with horrible bosses who are often demeaning. I believe any job can be a good job; it is what you make of it. But if you are going to do a job, why not grow, learn, and excel while you are there? I have not had one job where I did not try and excel and progress. From McDonald's in my teens to my current job as Vice President of Digital & Operations of Digital, I believe if you are going to spend most of your waking life there, you better make it count.

If you are a janitor, be the best janitor you can be. Make the place as clean as you can. If there are multiple janitors, try to become the team lead, captain, or manager. Better yet, eventually start your own janitorial services company and get your own clients.

From Rags To Riches

Richard Montanez, a Mexican immigrant, told Fox News Latino that growing up on his side of the tracks, aspirations among his community weren't very high. Most of the kids he knew hoped to get a job at the town's factory in Ontario, California. He struggled to learn English, dropped out of high school, and went to work as a janitor at the Frito-Lay plant in Rancho Cucamonga. His modest ambitions were "to drive the trash truck"—that is, until someone told him he could dream bigger. One day, the president of the company sent a video message to all employees. The message was direct and inspiring: "Act like an owner." Richard took that as an opportunity to "do something different."[27]

As the story goes, one day a machine broke down, and a batch of Cheetos did not get flavored, so Richard took the flavorless Cheetos home with him. Pulling from his Mexican roots and inspired by the men selling corn on the streets, Richard added Mexican spices, and Flaming Hot Cheetos were born. Richard eventually presented the idea to the Frito-Lay executives, who loved it, and now it is their number-one selling product line. Richard moved from janitor and wannabe trash truck driver to the Executive Vice President of Multicultural Sales and Community Activation for PepsiCo's North American divisions. Could Richard have stayed in his first position merely surviving, or was his life made better by deciding to thrive?

What I want everyone to realize is that while his other fellow coworkers made no changes, he decided, on the basis of one message from the CEO, to think and act differently, and his entire life changed. He found the "recipe" for success in his own life, and you can too. If he was of the mindset, *What do I know? I am uneducated. I can barely speak English. I am poor. I have a lowly job. Who would want to hear my ideas or listen to me?* then he would still be mopping floors and not leading a division of a Fortune 500 company. His idea was remarkably simple, but through the process, he had to learn to speak to executives, prepare a presentation, package his products, get a tie, and read books on selling. No one said it would be easy, but Richard applied himself and did his best. That is all anyone can do.

But you can see how easy it would have been for Richard to settle into a mundane life of factory work. This happens all the time. It is hard to better yourself. Therefore, not everyone is rich, famous, or well off. It is easier to allow gravity to keep you down than to take the amount of effort and force it takes to propel yourself upward.

27 Tania Luviano, "Our American Dream: The Janitor Who Invented Flamin' Hot" Fox News, March 2012 https://www.foxnews.com/world/our-american-dream-the-janitor-who-invented-flamin-hot-cheetos.

You may start to think to yourself, *That's just one man's story*, but there are many self-made men and women of all cultures and nationalities who stopped being ordinary and started being extraordinary. It just requires a pivot. A paradigm shift. A mental visualization of seeing more for yourself. You can be more, have more, do more, and dream more if you try.

Richard closed his Fox News video, saying, "Latinos who have made it like myself have a responsibility to open doors to younger generations and teach them that they can do it." He gives back time and money in scholarships because he knows what it is like to be hungry. Hunger inside can be the catalyst toward change. It motivates you if you are hungry enough to finally do something about it. You can be satisfied by a cheap, non-nutritious meal, or work a little harder to have a healthy, hearty, nutritious one. The cheap fast food will get you through but may cause a lot of other problems later, while eating healthy foods may take more time to prepare, but they promote vitality and longevity.

We love a rags-to-riches story, but each story is an inspiring motivator reminding us that anyone can change their life. Richard is not special. He is a regular person just like you and me. He is not a superhero; he came from very modest, humble beginnings. But he doesn't talk down about himself or say that he was nothing or nobody, or list all the things holding him back. He just progressed forward with the belief that he could do it, just like the aforementioned businessman with the fake John D. Rockefeller check in his safe. If you believe you can thrive, if you believe you can achieve, if you believe that you can be successful and have what you want, then you can.

JK Rowling: From Welfare To Winner

Before the money and the fame of Harry Potter, Joanne (aka JK Rowling) could have used a bit of magic in her own life. She was an unemployed single mother on public assistance who was clinically depressed and suicidal. She was struggling financially and laden with sadness. She was overwhelmed by failed jobs, failed relationships, and a crying newborn to care for. She thought she was "the biggest failure" she knew. At the time, she had just finished her first novel. She shopped it to multiple publishers; twelve rejected her, but the thirteenth took a small chance on her because she had decided to take a chance on herself. What magically turned JK Rowling into an international bestselling author and self-made billionaire with a book and movie franchise? In an *Inc.* magazine article, JK Rowling said, "I stopped pretending to myself that I was anything other than what I was and began to direct all my energy to finishing work that mattered to me." She had gained the determination to succeed where she "truly belonged." She overcame her fears and started believing in her "big idea." She concludes, "Rock bottom became a solid foundation on which I rebuilt my life."

Who has not been in dire straits with the faintest hope of recovery? But she recovered. She came from the bleakest of circumstances, like Richard, but there was one decision that separated them from those who achieve versus those who dream. Let's unpack what JK Rowling said earlier. First you must realize who you are:

You are great.
You are fearfully and wonderfully made.
You have everything inside you to achieve all your heart's desires.

But you must stop pretending or disbelieving in yourself, and it is hard, especially if you grew up in an environment where people told you that you can't. But you are grown now, and you can start telling yourself you can. JK Rowling directed her energy to not only starting but to finishing the work that fulfilled her. This is what separates a dream from a goal. If she had merely just started a book and never finished, we would never have heard of the orphan boy who had magic inside him but didn't know it, who lived under the worst of circumstances, to become the greatest wizard at Hogwarts.

I like how she says she succeeded where she "belonged." You can succeed anywhere, but the best success is where you want it to be. I could excel at my job, but if I am not passionate about it, then it is just busyness and not my business. Then JK Rowling overcame her worst fear "and survived" in the same way her character Harry survived from Voldemort. The stories and songs we write are often metaphors for what is happening in our own lives, as we tend to draw from our own personal experiences. Lastly, I like how she ends her quote about rock bottom. Many of us started from the bottom. The beauty of it is there is no other place to go but up.

When I hit rock bottom and was flat broke, that is when I started to learn about personal finance and educated myself. I may not have become a billionaire like JK Rowling, but I am well on my way. The point is, she didn't say, "When I have a billion dollars, then I will be successful and happy." She was fulfilled by finishing work that meant something to her. This is something anyone can accomplish and something that can be completely done on your own, on your own terms. She didn't say, "When I get my book published or when I sell 500 million copies, I will have made it." She made it the day she typed "The End" on her old typewriter.

The day Joanne changed to JK Rowling was the day she decided to start living differently. Having a baby to care for likely helped her to want to live for someone else, and to succeed. For many of you who have kids, this is important. My mom was a single mom for many years, and she worked hard rising in the ranks in corporate America, for the sake of having enough for her kid. Richard not only was able to help himself but help his community by developing scholarships. The success you create for yourself in turn can help so many others if you let it. Even becoming a beacon of light in the darkness and being able to say, "I didn't have much, but I believed in myself and worked hard and changed my circumstances and you can do it too" is very powerful. This is better shown through actions and not words.

The Harry Potter book did not fall out of the sky into JK Rowling's lap, and the Flaming Hot Cheetos didn't happen to arrive in the mail from FedEx to Richard in the factory. They each put action and intention into making their product, pitching their product, and all the other behind-the-scenes work of bettering themselves. I am sure every time a publisher said no, JK Rowling had to think and refine her pitch. And Richard learned a slew of new skills as he moved along his path to success.

Existing Is Not Living

You are here. You exist. But you don't really, truly live until you understand what you are living for. Many people have no higher purpose in life, and thus they are just blowing in the wind, going wherever life takes them, for better or worse, 'til death. Your parents gave you life, but now what you decide to make of it is up to you. Anderson Cooper, an outspoken news anchor and the son of heiress Gloria Vanderbilt (the great-granddaughter of American railroad tycoon Cornelius Vanderbilt), explained that before his mother died, she told him, "There's no trust fund." She herself had inherited about five million dollars but created her own fashion empire worth about two hundred million at her death. Cooper told Fast Company that an inheritance is a curse, and he might not have had the incentive to work if he'd been cushioned by family finances.

A butterfly, through the process of breaking out of its cocoon, gains the wing strength to be able to emerge and fly. If you see a butterfly struggling and decide to help do it for him, he will fall to the ground and eventually die. You were given a life, but no one ever said it was going to be easy. Mine certainly was not and continues to be a constant battle in which I gain new skills through every crisis and opportunity. It is in the trials by fire that we reveal our true colors and show what we are made of. Those who overcome will fare better than those who succumb to the pressures and demands this life can bring.

If you are merely existing, your why is not strong enough to push through the muck and the mire to succeed. I can attest that staying power comes from willingness to sacrifice, to succeed long after the feeling or desire to do the work has faded. You must learn to push through the tumult and the strife. If it were easy, everybody would be doing it. Everyone would have amazing lives. But that is a fantasy. In the real world, reality bites, stings, and kicks us in the teeth, and the only ones who emerge victoriously bludgeoned in battle, who have won, are those with true grit.

Grit: You Have To Fight For It

Author and TED speaker Angela Duckworth, in her best-selling book *Grit: The Power of Passion and Perseverance*, explains that "*grit is passion and perseverance for very long-term goals. Grit is having stamina. Grit is sticking with your future, day-in, day-out. Not just for the week, not just for the month, but for years. And working hard to make that future a reality. Grit is living life like it's a marathon and not a sprint.*"[28] I had grit before I even knew what true grit was.

Often in life it is easier to quit than to stick it out. It is easy to leave and harder to stay. Living your best life is not for the faint of heart. It is not for the weak-minded. Seventy-eight percent of U.S. workers, according to CareerBuilder, are living paycheck to paycheck. It is why, according to Yahoo Finance 70 percent of Americans have less than one thousand dollars in savings. According to the *Washington Post* and the latest *World Happiness Report,* Americans are increasingly unhappy.

The inalienable rights of life (existence), liberty, and the pursuit of happiness are ideals worth fighting for. I know that not all of us enjoy the quality of life, or freedoms that we could, but our founding forefathers never promised that we would have nice cars, or homes, or be happy. This is because we must actively work to achieve these things, and even if inherited we must work to maintain and keep these things.

In Excess

In *The Life-Changing Magic of Tidying Up*, Marie Kondo states, "The question of what you want to own is actually the question of how you want to live your life." When it comes down to it, if I were to go around my apartment and touch everything to see if it "sparks joy" in me, the answer for 90 percent of the stuff would be no. American life is full of excess compared to other countries where space is scarce. We could often live on much less. We could be happier with only a few possessions. We could survive on even less. Eighty percent of the world population lives on less than ten dollars a day. And 25 percent of the world lives without electricity. I am not saying you must relegate yourself to a substandard existence. On the contrary. I believe these three questions must be answered to start truly living: What brings me the most joy? What do I want to possess? How do I want to choose to live?

28 Angela Duckworth, "Grit is passion and perseverance for very long-term goals" https://www.passiton.com/inspirational-quotes/7407-grit-is-passion-and-perseverance-for-very

It is also important to note that you do not have to own or possess something to use it. When I want a nice staycation with my girlfriend at the beach, I can feel like a much richer man and rent an Airbnb for the weekend and enjoy it, without having to work hard to purchase a beach house (all my houses are beach houses, *wink wink*). According to the *Wall Street Journal*, Americans spend $1.2 trillion annually on non-essential goods; in other words, items they do not need.[29] It is reported that 12 percent of the world's population that lives in North America and Western Europe account for 60 percent of private consumption spending, according to the Worldwatch Institute. In Britain, research found that the average ten-year-old owns 238 toys but plays with just twelve daily, according to *The Telegraph*.[30] We do not use many of the possessions we have, and yet we still want more. Why is that? Because human beings are naturally acquisitive, meaning we have a deeply rooted desire to have more and more, for no reason other than we want it.

In personal finance, one of the first things you must teach someone is understanding a need versus a want. People often say, "I need a car," or "I need a house," or "I need this pair of shoes," but in actuality, if you didn't have a car you could lower your carbon footprint by walking, taking public transit, or sharing rides. You could rent a nice home or live with someone else. You may need a pair of shoes, but you could get them at a discount store or thrift shop instead of a department store or boutique shop. I would not say that overspending or overindulging is truly living or thriving either. Because often it leads to debt, stress, and having to work harder than we need to. With thriving, like anything else there is a balance, a homeostasis.

Our things have become status symbols. We buy things we don't need with money we don't have to impress people we don't even like. That is why you never see a U-Haul following a hearse! The liberty our

29 Mark Whitehouse, *Wallstreet Journal*, April 2011 https://www.wsj.com/amp/articles/BL-REB-13793?responsive=y.

30 Joshua Becker, "Becoming Minimalist" https://www.becomingminimalist.com/clutter-stats/.

forefathers had in mind might also have included freeing your mind of consumerism and stuff-itis.

The Walking Dead

When I think about zombies, I am instantly catapulted into thinking about Michael Jackson's landmark *Thriller* music video. The word "zombie" comes from Haitian folklore and speaks of a dead body brought back to life, often through black magic or sorcery. What we do not realise is that, too often in life, the dead walk among us, without passion, drive, hope, or purpose. It's like they are dead on the inside. You know what the difference between speaking to someone full of life, happy to be on this planet, looking forward to their best days, and to someone who is lifeless, depressed, mundane, and thinks their best days are behind them and the future looks bleak? The answer is their choices. They are choosing to live their best life.

Like Ezekiel in the Bible with his dry bones, fortunately where there once was death, it is possible to breathe the breath of life back into someone on the brink of an emotional or spiritual death. This has to do with connecting to one's purpose, why you are here on earth. Human beings need something to live for. As mentioned earlier, you need a why, otherwise you are just marking time until death.

Whether thirteen or eighty-three, you can still use the time you have left to walk in your purpose. One of my favorite musicians, Bill Withers, did not pick up the guitar or start making songs until in his thirties. Ray Kroc didn't start McDonald's until his fifties, and celebrity TV chef Julia Child didn't publish her first cookbook until her late forties. It is never too late. I know many of us get scared, then the years creep by. We believe that if we have not discovered what our life's work will be by twenty, thirty, or forty, we are most likely never going to, but that simply isn't true.

Many of you are already partially doing what you want to do, you just need to ramp up, and some of you stopped doing it and need to start again. Some of you have no idea what you want to do, but that just means it's time to start doing the self-reflection work to figure out what you want most. What are you doing with *the rest of your life*?

In AMC's *The Walking Dead*, character Hershel Greene, portrayed by

Scott Wilson, delivers one of the most poignant lines from the series, saying, "You step outside, you risk your life. You take a drink of water; you risk your life. And nowadays you breathe, and you risk your life. Every moment now, you don't have a choice. The only thing you can choose is what you're risking it for."[31]

Isn't it worth risking it all, going for broke, doing what makes you happiest and most fulfilled? Is it risky? Yes. Could it not work out? Yes. Could you go belly up? Totally. But think of the flipside. In the movie *It's A Wonderful Life*, James Stewart as George Bailey stars as a man who has given up his dreams and attempts to kill himself, but a guardian angel intervenes and shows him all the lives he has touched and how the world and his family and community would not be the same without his contributions. You don't need a suicide attempt or divine intervention to prove that what you do matters to those around you. It does! And doing work and hobbies that matter to you matter.

What Matters Most

Jeff Olson, author of *The Slight Edge*, summarizes this theory by saying, "The truth is, what you do matters. What you do today matters. What you do everyday matters. *Successful people just do the things that seem to make no difference in the act of doing them and they do them over and over and over until the compound effect kicks in.*"[32] The process of day in and day out trying, and constantly gaining feedback and refining your processes, help to give you that slight edge, measuring how close to your goals you have come or how far you need to still go.

When you invest in yourself by living out your dreams, purpose, and highest potential, you will enjoy the magic of compounding in the same way you would with money in a savings account. Though it may seem like these little things do not add up, they do in a phenomenal way.

31 Ella Kemp, "The Walking Dead: Chandler Riggs stresses the importance" NME March 2020 https://www.nme.com/news/tv/the-walking-dead-chandler-riggs-hershel-actor-self-isolation-speech-2628249.

32 Zach quoting *The Slight Edge* by Jeff Olson, "Four Pillar Freedom" https://fourpillarfreedom.com/the-slight-edge/.

I use the Acorns app to save incremental amounts of money by investing my "spare change." Their motto is brilliant: "From acorns, mighty oaks grow." Saving just one or three dollars per month can add up to thousands later. The Acorns company invests it in mutual funds, stocks, and bonds. In the same way, you're investing in yourself, and that will yield the dividends of a self-esteem boost, and the pride that comes with working toward your own fulfillment. But many Americans never get their act together to start saving or investing; they coast through life and a part of them is dead because they never breathed life into that aspect of themselves. *But you can start living today!* Every little bit you do toward your goals and dreams matters! You matter!

Answer These Questions:

1. What do you need to do to stop surviving and start thriving?
2. What does self-actualization look like to you?
3. How will you know when you have achieved it?

7.

Delegate, Don't Deliberate

> *"Are we limiting our success by not mastering the art of delegation? It's simply a matter of preparation meeting opportunity."* —Oprah Winfrey, billionaire media mogul

Does anyone recall the Disney movie *Mary Poppins*, where the lovable character Bert, played by Dick Van Dyke, appears in the very beginning as the one-man band? He is wearing a huge drum with cymbals, horns, and a bunch of other instruments, using every appendage to play, sing, and make a spectacle of himself as a street performer in London. That movie will always have a special place for me from my childhood. And it is a good visual representation of what it feels like to run your own music business, at least for me. Over the years, I have worn so many hats, and sometimes it can feel very isolating, lonely, and often overwhelming. I am sure all you budding entrepreneurs reading this will understand. Even if you are a stay-at-home mom or dad, you get this. There is so much to do and only one of you to go around. You are often pulled in so many different directions, like a cheap knock-off Stretch Armstrong, and yet you are stretched all out of shape but not yet broken.

When starting a new venture and you have no money, all you have is yourself. But as the business progresses, you might be in a position of wanting or needing to hire someone else, whether that be full time, part time, or even an unpaid intern. But who do you pick first, and what are the next steps? There is no right or wrong answer, but whatever you do, go slow. This is your baby, and you don't want to destroy your little seedling before it has had a chance to fully bloom by doing too much too soon.

Even while being a solopreneur, I knew I needed people. I had to have band members and music engineers to make my dream come true. But as we grew bigger, I eventually needed to create my own publishing company, record label, and then build a team of PR, a radio promoter, a booking agent, and more. I started organically through research and asking people I knew to find good help.

But before I get to my first hire, let me explain the beauty of doing everything yourself first. Doing it first allows you to know when you need someone else. I had to be my own PR and marketing rep as well as be my own administrative assistant. I know how to create a press release, find PR contacts, and send pitch emails. I know how to converse with bloggers and convince someone to take a chance on me and write my story. Before I was able to hire someone, I asked friends who knew about PR to help me, and they did it for free. I always like to exhaust my network before having to spend money externally. If I had positioned myself correctly, I would have tried to find an intern, but I was at a point in my career where I did not want to work with someone who was learning. I wanted someone who could teach me, so that didn't work for my situation. But it certainly could work for you to hire an intern; I am still open to revisiting that option down the road, because it is very rewarding to give someone meaningful work, to help them get their feet wet in the industry, while also saving on labor costs.

I also learned how to refine certain processes and make improvements as I went along. My current boss likes to do a lot of things first himself, so he knows what he is passing off. This way he knows the pain points of doing that job and understands what resources a person needs to succeed in it.

Be careful if you have issues delegating and you are afraid to release the reins to someone else. I was reading a Q & A in *Success* magazine by Tony Jeary, aka "The Results Guy," that said that the fear of delegating is often being afraid that someone else will make a mistake. But you could also make more mistakes by not seeking the help you need sooner. Plus, eventually the work becomes too much for one person and if *you* only work, you don't own a business, you own a job.

Tony also made another great point—that a lot of fear can be mitigated if you make sure the person you delegate to gives you periodic updates on the project. One of my biggest pet peeves is being left wondering, *Where are we on that?* and I cannot get a hold of the person. As Tony says, "*Make it the delegate's responsibility to follow up, and you will save tons of time and have more peace of mind.*"

The First Hire

The first company I hired to assist my business was a PR agency. As Bill Gates once said, "If I was down to the last dollar of my marketing budget, I'd spend it on PR." If no one knows who you are, what you do, or that you exist, then you could have the best product or service and get nowhere with it. I had a chance meeting in a bar in Weho (West Hollywood) that put me in touch with a small boutique PR firm in Mid-Wilshire. After many years of writing my own press releases and finding my own press, now I had a team, which ended up being instrumental in hosting my successful release party for *The Gospel According to Cliff Beach* at Harvelle's in Santa Monica in 2017.

One of the biggest takeaways from that night was creating my own step and repeat (event banner) and red carpet for photos in front of the venue. That helped elevate my status, as cars and patrons walking by noticed that something big was happening. The PR agency also did a lot to raise my online PR profile by having me attend numerous red-carpet engagements in Los Angeles, Hollywood, and Beverly Hills. I finally had photos taken by Getty Images while being interviewed as a celebrity in my own right. They also helped me to get written interviews on blogs and have my event added to the major calendars for music and events in LA.

As a result of heavily promoting our show, we performed two sets to a packed house, captured the night with photos and video, created a cool Snapchat filter for social sharing, and earned four times in bonuses from the bar for high sales, while also selling quite a few of our new vinyl record. All of this would have been much harder to do without a small team to help. I have continued to work with this agency over the years and have also branched out to working with other agencies because they all specialize in different functional areas. With my current PR regime, we can find outlets to do exclusive premieres for my audio and video releases.

Working with the agencies has afforded me a tremendous learning opportunity to understand the news cycle, how to structure a PR campaign, and how to create space and time for these launches. I was always alone as an indie artist, working against the clock, being more reactive than proactive, and not getting as far ahead as I could have with the benefit of someone else's knowledge and contacts.

But hiring someone does not solve all your problems. I am still just as involved in my career as I have always been. Working as a team requires a lot of back and forth, follow-up calls, and emails. Just because you delegate to someone, you are still driving the bus. It also costs money up front, so when looking to add someone, you have to realise it is an investment in them, and you must make sure that you are aligned on goals and have realistic expectations and deadlines for execution. You must also try to negotiate the best deal possible for yourself, knowing how much you are willing to spend ahead of time and having them work within your budget. This means you may need multiple referrals and spend time shopping around. I found both of my PR agencies via word of mouth from a friend or another business partner. It is always best to find someone tried and true, although I am not opposed to finding someone who has the drive and needs the experience, because a less expensive deal could be made when they are just starting out and you are willing to be their first "trial run."

In hindsight, I would have looked for a PR agency sooner, but I always thought it was cost prohibitive. By not doing so, I lost some opportunities. I decided not to have a famous guest star on my album because I was told by a colleague there was no point to do it without PR, not realising that by the time the album was set to be released, I would have PR in place. That could have moved the needle forward a bit more. So I have learned to try to say yes more than no, believing that I can figure out what needs to get done on the back end, even if I do not have all of the things in place at the start. Don't think, *I can't*. Think, *How can I?*

Who are you thinking would help most as your first hire? Could it be someone for basic part-time assistance? Is it someone who can be virtual/remote, or do you need someone physically there? Start by writing a list of the low-level work that is taking up your time that you could shift to someone else, then figure out what tapping into a bigger network would do for you. What are you not good at or hate to do that you would be happy to take off your plate? The goal is to move as many things off your plate as possible—to free time, energy, and resources in order to focus as much effort as possible on money-making opportunities or the things that make you the happiest.

Expanding The Team

The next hire was a big win for me, and I hadn't even known it was possible. I had been a longtime fan of Daptone Records, an independent funk/soul record label based in Brooklyn, New York. They are pioneers in the business, with successful acts like Sharon Jones and The Dap Kings and Charles Bradley (RIP to both, gone too soon). I had always wanted to work with them, but they are very selective and primarily work with East Coast acts, so I thought about what the next best thing would be. I researched who they used to promote their records and stumbled upon the radio promotion team that they used, which, through some cold emails and cold calls, eventually became my radio promotion team.

Often in life, learning the best practices from someone further up the road saves you a lot of time, money, pain, and heartache. The radio team I use has a digital releasing and reporting system that is far better than what I could have done by myself. Through very hard work, they were able (in one year!) to get me one of my biggest milestones, being played on KCRW, a premiere tastemaker NPR music station based out of Santa Monica, California, a stone's throw from my apartment on the Westside. I had tried for over a decade to make that happen for myself, and though I had hit many other milestones, this was a huge win for me. All these things were a culmination of hard work and strategy that helped add legitimacy to my project.

For those of you not in music, you must figure out who your Daptone is and who you need to poach to work with. Who is someone you admire who you can emulate? Who works for them? Once you start researching and poking around, you start to notice that a lot of businesses use the same people. In the beauty world, often the manufacturers for one big product work for their competitors. It was the same when I was in the fashion and shoe apparel industry. Even if you must start small and work your way up, you can start to know who it is you need to eventually work with and then start networking your way up.

I was fortunate to add on a booking agent a few years ago based out of Las Vegas. A lot of milestones also hit there. They were able to secure me several dates at a five-star hotel; got me my first *Fox News* morning show guest spot; and eventually helped me get my first Ticketmaster event, headlining at a club inside Rio Vegas. I am always humbled and very appreciative of all the hard work to pitch my band, and so thankful for a good friend who worked with the agency at Caesar's Palace for connecting me with them. But it was a relationship I had to nurture for over a year before I saw any movement. It takes patience and it takes time, which I know can be disheartening, especially as we get up in age; but it is never too late, and good things come to those who are patient. You don't want to rush. Take your time to vet the people you are going to be working with. These relationships could last several years, and you are trusting them to work for you and represent you, so doing your due diligence is a must.

One of the hardest areas I have struggled to partner with is a good licensing agency. At one point, I was referred by the radio team to a licensing company in San Francisco that didn't do much, as they were busy with their full roster. But recently, through two other collaborations, I have been able to sign with two new firms. I always have the belief that the next time can work out even if the last time didn't. Every year I get a little bit better at my craft and telling my story. And licensing is a waiting game anyway, as you must wait for the right opportunity for the right song in your catalog, and the royalties can take years to roll in. I was mentored once by the artist Akon on a radio program called Business Rockstars; he told me that licensed song royalties are your retirement money. The main point is to keep and get the best team that you can afford to get as early on as possible. It is a long game that pays off in the long run.

The last component I added to my business recently is physical distribution. I have had an online distribution company for a number of years, but this was an additional relationship that I had wanted; if I had more foresight, I would have added it when I released my vinyl record in 2017, but I didn't decide to create my label until 2018. Again, it was another series of cold emails and phone calls, this time based on learning what another indie label, Colemine Records, was doing. I knew that a lot of their artists were being distributed through Fat Beats, so I decided for my next two releases I was going to try and work with them. I tried retroactively to do my 2017 release, but that was in late 2018 or early 2019, and the album cycle had passed. It is okay, though. I am a firm believer that whatever doesn't make it into this batch can make it into the next. I have the same approach in songwriting—there will be more albums, there will be more songs. So we struck a deal to work together in 2020.

The same can be true for you. If you cannot afford to bring anyone on full time or part time, sometimes even using ad hoc, one-off projects like Upwork or Fiverr can be instrumental in propelling you forward. I have used this approach to get Spotify playlist contacts, submissions, and a handful of other low-level tasks. You must think outside of the box. For those struggling with cash, bartering for a friend's or relative's help, or having a significant other help or a kid or intern can be a good idea. Try not to think from a place of "How can I afford this?" as much as "Can I afford not to?" and even still, "How can I make this possible for myself?" There is always a way; we just must sometimes have to wrack our brains for the answer.

Adding these people has saved me tons of time and added years back to my life. I wish I had done it sooner in some ways, though all things come together in their own time. I would encourage you to just start exploring the possibility of adding someone on or some service to help with minor things, so that you can get down to business.

Wish List

I love to keep a wish list of what I would love to have in the future. It could be a hope list or a dream list, but for me it basically is what I know I want or need but do not know exactly how I can make it a reality. For instance, the next delegation that I have been working on in the last year is securing a personal manager for my musical endeavors. I have been courting a person who is interested and has many years of experience managing a five-time Grammy–Award-winning artist in a related genre. With a lot of things in my industry, it comes down to bandwidth and timing. This is once again a relationship I started from a cold email/phone call, which brings me to an important point. Most of what it takes to succeed in your business is not being the smartest but being hard working. Paraphrasing motivational speaker and author Gary Vaynerchuck, *"I may not be the smartest person in the room, but no one will out-hustle me."* I respect that. I had no contacts in my industry, and I had to work hard to get everyone from my wish list. You can find the right people and right mix you need; you just have to look.

In my day gig, I often wish for a bigger team and keep a running list of what I would get if resources and budget allowed. Often in these jobs I start as a one-person department and expand, growing a team under me. I have managed up to fourteen at one time, currently five, plus some external agency partners. I am always looking to free up my time so that I can work on higher-level tasks that need my full attention. The less I am involved in the weeds and the minutiae, the better for me and the company.

There are people naturally better at certain processes, systems, and software, or those who are way more proficient in a certain subject matter and expertise; I am happy to find, cultivate, and grow a team organically. Having a wish list helps, but it does not make you a good leader or manager. Oftentimes, by running your own show, you may have a hard time communicating what you want to a team. I think this is a good skill to cultivate. Any business or endeavor that wants to scale or continue to grow will need people in some way.

As you start dreaming and adding to your wish list, think of it as if you had a magic lamp and a genie inside was able to expand your team. Who do you know today who, if you had the money, you would hire? Who do your competitors use whom you could also benefit from? Give yourself the gift of thinking about who you need now so you can start seeking them out and adding on as soon as you are able to.

I think it is a good idea to write this down on paper or digitally. I keep so many notes in my iPhone, as I am always thinking and plotting my next move. It comes down to the law of attraction again. Think about when you get a new car, you never noticed that brand of car on the road as much, and now you are starting to see it everywhere. A wish list is just like that new car. By starting to lock your sights on what you need, like on a vision board, even if you don't know how you will get it, you will start to welcome the possibilities and the universe will start sending things your way.

When I added on team members, I knew all the steps necessary to make a music project run, and slowly I started to build that team from that wish list. At each mark I always asked friends and business associates for referrals and continue to do so. Word of mouth marketing is the best form of marketing because a real testimonial on how they performed for someone else is a good indicator of how it might be to work with them, it is not always an exact science, but a personal recommendation carries more weight than just hearing what they have to say about themselves.

I find often when I am explaining to my mentees about the wish list, they wish they had made it sooner. I want to explain that it is not like a normal wish list, where you dream and make no action steps behind it. You must write these things down and start researching how much they cost. Ask yourself, *Do I need to pay upfront for this service? Who are others using? Can I bundle services for a better rate? Can I combine with someone else and share the cost of the service?* As you start to make questions about each wish list item and start doing your research, you will start to see that many things you thought were out of reach were actually right there in front of you. You just have to stretch to get them.

For example, before joining the National Academy for Recording Arts and Sciences (NARAS) as a voting member (they're owners of the Grammys), I didn't think that it was possible. I thought I'd have to be more established and backed by a bigger label to join. I happened to run into a non-voting member who explained they had different levels and that you could also be sponsored by someone to join and I should apply. From that one conversation, I logged on to their website, saw the criteria, and, when I had enough commercially released material, I submitted and was approved. All that time I thought it was out of reach, but it was not as far out as I had originally thought. Also, I thought it was harder than it actually was, but I had never done any research to see how feasible it was because of a falsely preconceived notion that I had to be "bigger" to do it. What I had to be was strategic and diligent. That is the benefit of creating the wish list and then doing your due diligence research. You can achieve it if you believe it and go after it with all your might.

Digital Tools And Automation

We are fortunate now to live in a digital age where we can use a variety of tools to make our lives simpler. Some people are apprehensive or just extremely late adopters to new tech, but I believe technology should be your friend, not your enemy. It does not fully replace some of the old school approaches, but in many ways enhances how you do business and operate, personally and professionally. Depending on your business/side hustle, some may be more niche or relevant than others, but I think you can benefit from the following functional areas and tools that I have used as the Vice President of Digital & Operations at my current company and in my side business.

Social Media Management

If you don't exist on social media to some degree, and over several platforms, in many ways you don't exist in the eyes of people who want to connect with you. I personally have a Facebook profile and fan page, Twitter, Instagram, YouTube, and LinkedIn accounts. Posting, engaging, responding, and staying active can be very time consuming and exhausting. Instead of letting this take up more time than it should, investigate a management tool such as Later or Hootsuite to monitor, schedule, interact, and engage using a dashboard to review analytics and progress.

Photo-Creation Software

Hiring a graphic designer is always best, if you can afford it, but sometimes you need something amazingly simple and easy that you can do yourself. I have used Canva app, or Canva.com, to create social media posts, album artwork, animated GIFS, and much more. It is fun and very easy to use, with tons of free and cheap stock images and a very convenient dashboard that stores all of your content to make it easy to post or download to your phone or computer.

Cloud File Storage

I find it very convenient to have one place to store all my files in the cloud, to send links to share across the internet at the click of a button. I have used iCloud, Google Drive, One Drive, WeTransfer+, and Dropbox, among others, to store files over the last ten years. It is a great way to safeguard your large files, back up files, and have access on the go without having to carry large external hard drives. Many storage sites offer free solutions with ridiculously cheap upgrades for larger storage.

Video Conferencing

In the post-COVID years, we will not remember a time when we did not have Zoom virtual meetings. I conducted several video calls, recorded webinars, and performed live showcases using the platform in 2020. It is very affordable, with the capability of scaling easily and offers cloud storage in paid versions to save video, audio, and chats to recall and share via recap emails, YouTube links, and more.

Email Marketing

For any small business, if you want a sure-fire way of being able to track and make sure customers are getting your messages, email is still king. I have used several platforms like MailChimp and Constant Contact to design, send, and review analytics for my email newsletters for both work and my side hustle. What I love most about this is being able to see who opened the emails to adjust my text and photos, as well as having very easy-to-use-templates. For a bonus, I like to review other companies and what they are emailing, using tools like milled.com too.

Accounting Software

If there is one area you cannot afford to make mistakes in your business early on, it is accounting and taxes. The last thing you want is an audit. An online tool like Xero will make it easier in the beginning to be your own bookkeeper; it helps with tracking expenses, profits, debts, sending invoices, and collecting payments, and offers an extremely simple platform. Your tax person will thank you. If you are your own tax person, you will be thanking yourself.

Tax Software

I have used TurboTax for a few years to e-file my taxes. What I love most is how the software walks you through all the business deductions, shows you your audit risk, and allows you to e-file both state and federal together for one low fee. It costs me way less doing it myself, even with a complex tax situation, than having someone else do it for me, so this software has been a life saver. Plus, whenever I need it, I can review and download these files. It also has file storage to scan documents in order to make filling out forms faster or to review later.

Website

If you are doing any e-commerce for physical products, you will need at least a basic informational website. I use Bandzoogle, which is specifically for music, but Shopify is quite easy to use for e-commerce. All the website tools have access to analytics, which are powerful for any business, and templates to be able to get your site up and running quickly and easily. I think anyone promoting a business or even some hobbies can benefit from having a website, especially as it relates to SEO and Google. It is your calling card.

To launch and maintain a website in your area of interest, start by reading blog articles or searching on Google. The main takeaway is that technology should be another tool that helps you realize your dream faster and easier. So many businesses have created software and apps that will save you time, money, and frustration. It will be trial and error figuring out what works for you based on the cost and benefit, but luckily almost all allow some type of trial before you buy, or have ample reviews and articles on their performance so that you can make an informed decision.

What To Do With This Freed-Up Time?

For many of us, more time is a luxury that we cannot afford. With so many responsibilities, from work to school to family and social obligations, taking on a side hustle can be an arduous task. We often have no idea how much time we waste. David Finkel, author of *The Freedom Formula*, said in a 2018 article in *Inc.* magazine that in a forty-hour-plus work week, over half, or 21.8 hours is wasted.

The sad thing is, like many of us, David's clients "don't have the time to do the things that they know they want to and need to do in their business." In the *Harvard Business Review* study quoting the Covey Center for Leadership Study, they found, after surveying more than four hundred executives, that most have a seventy-two-hour work week versus forty. In a Gallup Poll made jointly with Wells Fargo, they say 57 percent of small-business owners work six days a week and over 20 percent work seven days a week.

But more importantly in David's own study, he found that 30 percent of our workweeks represents low- to no-value work, referring to activities that can be delegated for fifty dollars an hour or less to someone else to free up time. They equated this to about 6.8 hours a week, almost one full workday. Further, the article says 3.4 hours a week go to low-value emails, 3.2 hours to low-value interruptions, 1.8 hours to low-level requests from coworkers, with another 1.8 hours on "putting out preventable fires." The last of the time wasters is over one hour a week on nonproductive meetings, as evidenced in Cameron Herold's book *Meetings Suck*.

Some of this problem can be attributed to poor time management. So what tools are available to help mitigate and improve these processes for you? Many tools allow you to schedule in advance and automate. Also, tools like Fiverr or Upwork help you to find cheaper labor. In my job, we used several outsourced virtual assistants to help with lower-level tasks. I once read of a man who outsourced thirty-eight hours of his 250 thousand dollar a year job to only work two hours a week! It helped him improve his health, work productivity, and eventually he created a business as an efficiency expert trainer.

So, I ask again, what could you do with all this time? Well, first you could *not* work seven days a week; keep it to five so that your overall weekly hours are around forty. Tim Ferris touts a four-hour work week! All things are possible. How much more time could you spend relaxing, playing, spending time with family, and doing other things that you enjoy with delegation and using digital tools?

It is not going to be a magic pill, where every aspect of your life is fixed all at once, but once you are aware of it, you can start to think and act differently to try and make your life easier and more manageable. I think intuitively we know that some things are time vampires, sucking precious time and energy out of us and yielding little to nothing in return.

Whatever you decide to do with this free time, use it wisely. For some of you it will create much needed downtime for rest, relaxation, and rejuvenation. A time to meditate, commune, and restore. For others it may free up time for personal development, hobbies, or recreation.

There is no right or wrong way to use the time if you are making a conscious decision on how best to use it. Every moment of every minute counts. Shahenshah Hafeez Khan warns,

> *"Free time allows building of reputations, either as someone who is excellent at killing time by doing nothing, or someone who can utilize the time by creating things out of nothing. People who become habitual [at] doing nothing, get nothing at the end."*

I choose to be the one creating something and not the one with nothing to show for it, and I want the same for you.

In the end, like everything else mentioned, it all comes down to living with more intentionality. Living each day with purpose, each moment hitting a milestone. Intentional living allows for better uses of your time, for a higher level of work, and for personal or spiritual development. Those who waste time will lose it, and those who use their time wisely will find more of it. Don't waste time on activities best suited for delegation. Start delegating as soon as you are able.

Wish I Delegated Earlier

Some people are natural delegators, while some abhor delegation, and the rest of us fall on a scale somewhere in between. Whenever

I can assign a task or responsibility to someone else, I am happy to. Sometimes, for lack of resources, funds, or wanting to maintain control, I did not delegate. Looking back, I wished I had not only done it, but that I had done it sooner. In order to delegate effectively, you must know there are no right or wrong ways, simply different ways, and oftentimes there are multiple paths to get you there. You cannot be attached to "the way we have always done it." You must be open-minded. You must create new habits and routines. With delegation you must be noticeably clear on expectations, with lots of check-ins to monitor progress. You must have faith in who you have entrusted. You must plan out your time and have a checklist for to-dos with your delegates.

Building A Diverse Team

Some people also associate busyness with productivity, but there is a difference between busy work and getting results. You must become solution- and results-focused. Whenever I create teams, I let them take full ownership of their work, which makes them value the outcome more and act more responsibly. I, like them, also like to work autonomously and do not like to be micromanaged. I had a manager once who said he did not micromanage, he just "fostered an environment where his team could produce their best work."

Not only would delegating earlier have helped me be further along in my career and side hustle, but it would also have saved me a lot of stress. It's in my nature to take on multiple projects, overloading my schedule until I reach my breaking point and beyond. As a result, I often end up doing myself a disservice. Not only do I risk collapsing from exhaustion and fatigue, but I also do not benefit from the knowledge, expertise, and networks of others. I have also found that having a diverse mix in delegation is great—building a team of people from various backgrounds, cultures, and points of view. Statistically, diverse teams outperform homogeneous ones. Not only does diversity help to curtail groupthink and encourage new ideas, but diverse teams tend to be more resilient due to the different mixes of personalities, emotions, and experiences. They also can be more prone to innovation. Again, by having other educational and cultural backgrounds, you fare better than those who come from similar situations.

You Cannot Do It All

Ilya Pozin (founder of Pluto TV), in an *Inc.* magazine article titled "10 Quotes That Will Make You Think Like the Best Entrepreneurs," wrote, "*The sooner you learn to delegate, the sooner you'll rise to the top. No entrepreneur can do it all. Those who understand how to depend on others will succeed.*" She was inspired in her article by Bill Gates, who was quoted as saying, "As we look ahead into the next century, leaders will be those who empower others."

Empowering others does not limit or diminish your personal power; instead, it enhances it exponentially. Some people think delegation lowers their self-worth, or perhaps it simply triggers their ego. It is hubris to think you can do it all. Just like many believe the best way to make money is with other people's money, the best way to manage time is to use someone else's. Time is scarce. In the end, you need to spend your time on what brings you the highest value. Danny Iny, in an article for *Inc.* magazine, warns that "time is finite. So when you trade time for money, you cap your income. Whether you are paid fifteen or one hundred and fifty dollars, your income is limited by the number of hours you can put in." Just like financing with debt, or through investor capital, delegation allows you access to infinite human resources. The idea is to become limitless. Limitless in your reach, limitless in your potential, limitless in your time, and limitless in your abilities. It takes delegation to other people to make that possible. You start to own a business and not a job. As I mentioned earlier, you own it; it does not own you.

We cannot go back and change the past; we can only make different key decisions to influence and elevate our future. If you had any negative thoughts about delegation, or previous bad experiences with it, it is time to put those out of your mind and start to make new memories.

I want you to start thinking limitlessly. You need to delegate. If someone else can do the low-value work for less than your hourly wage for your work, you should pass it off because your time is better spent making more money or doing what you want to do. Once you get into the habit and routine of delegating, like anything else, it will become easier. You will not get the hang of it right away. Some things may slip through the cracks, and you may lose visibility for a time on some projects, but all these things can be corrected in due time. I am confident that with a little practice and patience, you will be a delegation master in no time flat.

Answer These Questions:

1. What are some low-level tasks you could get off your plate today?
2. If you did not have these tasks on your plate, where else could you better allocate your time?
3. What trust issues keep you from delegating?
4. What financial issues keep you from delegating?

8.

Self-Employment and Self-Care

> *"When you see yourself as self-employed, you develop the entrepreneur mentality. The mentality of the highly independent, self-responsible, self-starting individual. You see yourself as completely in charge of your physical health, your financial well-being, your career, your relationships, your home, your car, and every element of your existence. This is the mindset of the truly excellent person."*
> —Brian Tracy, best selling author

Whether you work for someone else or you are self-employed, you always end up working for yourself. If you go to work for someone else, though, you will not have enough intrinsic motivation to perform at your optimal performance level. You must get into the mindset that you work for yourself, even if you are paid by someone else. *Where do I want to be? What do I want to accomplish? What is in my direct control? What problems can I solve? How can I become better?* These are questions you should be constantly asking yourself.

Then you need to shift your thinking: *What is my exit strategy? Do I want to work for this employer forever, or do I want to start my own thing? Could I do this same thing but by myself instead? Have I learned enough to hang out my shingle?*

Over the years, I have worked for multiple music schools: one at a Korean church, one at a Japanese Music House, at two storefront music shops, and another that had private lessons for students in bands. I have taught at facilities and in people's homes. By the end of my tenure, I realized that the school was great at getting me students, but they took half the pay for administration, branding, and overhead expenses. I could make double that by finding my own clients, and I could charge more traveling to them for convenience, which meant no overhead for me. Plus, I would be able to have more flexibility in my hours and days and be more selective about the students I taught.

Many of us in the gig economy working for Uber Eats, Postmates, Jolt, and all the other delivery services enjoy being able to make our own schedules. But those who work for those services must take care of their own car; they don't have a choice of customers and don't get to pick the best routes for delivery.

You need to figure out when to jump ship and start your own thing, just as I did. If you have hit a wall or ceiling, where there is nowhere else to go in your current job, you will need to find another job, start your own thing, or renegotiate your current deal to make it work for you.

Gone are the days of working at the same place for forty years, retiring with a party and a gold watch. That level of loyalty is gone. You have to wake up every morning with the feeling that you are going to gain as much valuable experience on the job, while continuing to add value to your firm to get promoted, while also keeping your eyes on the prize of your other dreams and aspirations.

I have worked in the corporate world for almost twenty years, and it has never been a secret at any of those jobs that my passion was music and that I did lots of personal projects on my own time. I think most firms realize that it is an asset, not a liability, that workers should have other things outside of work that fulfill them. For me, it has helped to cultivate and foster more creativity at work. I have been able to inject my creativity into projects that might otherwise be ordinary as a way to make them more fun, but also to make them more interesting and productive.

As my side businesses have expanded into creating more content, learning about real estate, and other business opportunities, I have been able to stay afloat by making my day gig more manageable. I've moved up to a point where I could work remotely and create my own schedule as needed. I understand not everyone will be able to do this, and this took me many years to master, but I believe all lives can be curated to some degree with a little bit of effort and a whole lot of trust. I have been able to work independently and get more things done for myself and my company, which has allowed me to continue to curate a workflow that works best for me. Had I not been able to produce, I would not have been afforded this luxury.

Work On What Really Matters Most

Working for yourself simply means you work on what matters most to you. You are taking full responsibility for the outcomes of your work. It may seem like you are working for your boss or your clients or customers, but ultimately it is for you. You want to become better. You want to work hard. You want to earn and be rewarded and recognized for your efforts. But the main objective is to do it on your own terms. You want to be able to call your own shots.

The best way to be able to work for yourself is to first work on yourself, and that takes preparation. When I was starting out in the working world, I needed more management. I didn't know what I was doing and didn't feel confident to make decisions 100 percent on my own. But just as a baby bird eventually must be kicked out of the nest and learn to fly on its own, you also have to be raised up to eventually think more for yourself. In fact, in the wild, if a mama bird kicks her baby out of the nest and it drops to the ground, she will only swoop in a few times to save it before letting it fall. In the wild, animals know that eventually they must take care of themselves. For us in the working wild, it can be a jungle out there too. And your boss is not going to be able to swoop in and save the day in every email, at every meeting, and in every second of the day. Eventually the ball is going to be in your court, and you are going to have to run with it. That is why we work hard to prepare for when this day comes so that we will be more than ready for it. That is the day you can fully realize what it means to work for yourself. You must take care of that customer. You must give that presentation. You must put out that fire. That is why everyone who is smart at work realizes that whether you work for someone else or you work for yourself, you ultimately work for *you*.

Put Work In Maintenance Mode

If your work situation is not a place of fulfillment, it is important to find a way to avoid focusing more time and energy than you need to. If you are not trying to advance and climb the corporate ladder, it is okay to simply maintain the status quo while you pursue your real dreams and passion. For some of us, it is more difficult than others. People who perform manual labor or have demanding work hours can feel drained. Finding the energy to explore these ideas can be downright exhausting. But every job, if you have been doing it a long time, starts to create a rhythm and a routine, and once you recognize and fall into it, it can become a little bit easier to manage.

Currently, in my day job, within the confines of a nine-to-five, I can extend and move those hours earlier or later to allow for other things I need to do during the day. During my working hours, I have learned how to maintain while not decreasing work output by keeping a to-do list and doing three to five major tasks per day. Trying to put too many tasks on your plate will eventually have you overloaded. Your mind and body can only handle so much at once. Studies also show that we are not good at multitasking; we actually produce more when working on one dedicated task at a time. Many people have a variety of methods of accomplishing tasks—some do the hardest or most important task first, while others like to do two or three smaller tasks to be able to check them off early.

There is no right or wrong way, but when planning how you will structure your work day, it is imperative that you think about how to do enough to get by, while leaving more time and energy for things that keep you happy. Maintenance mode also refers to better utilization of work downtime. There are natural lulls in the work; some days you will work more than others. On those days that you have less work to do, you can use that time more efficiently. I work in front of a computer all day, so while I am waiting for someone to get back to me on something (and I cannot continue without their approval), I will take that time to educate myself on things that would benefit both my company and my business. There is a lot of overlap, since everything that I learn on the job for digital marketing and e-commerce directly translates to anything I do in my side business. For some, the overlap may not be there or may not be as much, but if you get extra time to read, write, or research something, then that is a better use of your time than doing nothing or low-value work.

I used to work years ago for a large shoe company in their mail room. In between mail runs, if someone needed me to wait on picking up a package they needed to mail out, I would work on songs while sitting in my work van. I would write down lyrics in my notepad, which evolved later to my iPhone notes, while listening to producer's tracks to write top-line melodies and lyrics. I also recorded voice memos for song ideas to work on when I got home. I distinctly remember so many songs that started out that way, often going back to those old notes and voice memos for inspiration. I may have had only five or ten minutes here and there, but I could easily put my work on hold in those lulls and get back to what really drives me. Even if you took five minutes to meditate, you would feel more refreshed and centered coming back to work than goofing off for five minutes while waiting for a call, email, or for someone to drop something off.

According to an article on upkeep.com, did you know that there are eighteen types of maintenance to keep up with the upkeep of systems and equipment, or to extend something's use or lifecycle? (read more at https://www.onupkeep.com/learning/maintenance-types.) Companies often implement several in their maintenance goals. The reason we try to maintain is to keep everything in the best condition, with minimal effort to prevent breaking down, so that its usefulness lasts longer. This is what you want. You want to be able to keep the day job you have without having to worry about it, while you work your butt off on your side project and goals. In maintaining, like anything else, you are either proactive or reactive. Like the adage says, "The best defense is a good offense." You need to learn how to maintain way before anyone at work ever asks you to. The entire point of maintenance mode is to work behind the scenes while everyone is doing something else. No one should really sense that you are doing anything different. You still show up on time and leave on time. You still contribute, but only to the point that makes sense. No less, no extra. Some people (like me) are natural overachievers, so they may find this difficult, but they will soon learn it is perfectly normal to just do and be "enough."

When you are maintaining, you are keeping all the wheels in motion, the balls in the air, doing just enough to keep your day gig happy, while feverishly working on anything that you are passionate about. If you can bring more of your passion into your job, even better. I have pulled creative ideas from my side hustle and used them in my day job. Not every job will be conducive to this, but I am a firm believer that you can do it. I have seen people bring in meditation, cooking, book clubs, public speaking classes, happiness experts, massage clinics, chiropractors, and other types of wellness into the workplace from their outside activities to bring some of their outside passions inside. Some people start a work sports team, such as kickball, softball, or basketball, to round out their work week. This not only helps maintain good morale but can also lead to more divergent thinking, which can be very helpful when teams get stuck on problems too.

Nine-To-Five, Then Bye

I try to keep a picture of Fred Flintstone sliding down the dinosaur's back as he hears the bird (bell) whistle, signifying it's quitting time, with his signature "Yabadabadoo!" as I head home from work Monday through Friday. Fred is excited to go home after a long day at the rock quarry. When my day gig ends, that is when my night job begins. This is my time. I have eight hours of sleep, eight hours of my day job, and eight hours of whatever I choose. Could it really be that simple? Of course not. Sometimes work takes more than eight hours. Plus, there are meals, showers, exercise, errands, social activities, doctor's appointments, and many other tasks that must get done in the day. Some of us also have long commutes or family commitments or second jobs, either full or part time.

I, like many of you, have all these things. So that eight hours a day dwindles down to maybe two or three. If I allow work to bleed over too much, then it becomes one or two. If I am not careful and I let phone calls or TV take up too much time, then none of what I needed to get done that day gets done, and that is bad. As I write this, I have worked all day, exercised, and attended my public speaking group. I had a phone call with my girlfriend and then turned on the computer to write for one hour before bed. This is a normal day. Even if I still get after-hours texts or emails from work, I try to keep most of my day work limited to nine-to-five so that *my time* really is my time.

I have the luxury of being able to borrow time from my day job, so if I need to do something non-work-related during those hours, I can, and then I just make up the time during a different part of the day. Sometimes when I cannot sleep, I get an early or late jump on the day starting at five a.m. or working until eleven p.m., which frees up my daytime hours for personal work or extra sleep (I love taking naps). But that is the exception, not the rule. I prefer to keep normal hours for my day gig, leaving the evenings and weekends for all my personal projects.

We will get to this more in the work-life balance chapter, but keeping your work relegated to nine-to-five is particularly important because you need to have boundaries. If people feel you are on call twenty-four seven, you will not be able to shut on and off the part of you at work. It is even more imperative to create that space or separation from work and home now because many of us are working from home.

For some, the issue is boundaries, but often the problem has to do with how we schedule our day. By not managing time as effectively as possible, you might end up working longer hours to get everything done. Here are some things you can do to combat this challenge:

Have a Timed Agenda for Meetings: When running or organizing a meeting, it is imperative to have a timed agenda. In Toastmasters, we meet once a week, every Tuesday from seven to nine p.m. We have a timed agenda with a segment for our business meeting, then the three main sections, and room at the end for wrap-up. Each subsection is assigned a person to manage that part of the meeting, with timing up to the minute. Our meetings start and end on time, and we have a timer who holds up colored cards to indicate how much time is left for each section so we know when to stop and move on.

Minimize Interruptions: Gloria Mark, a professor who studies Digital Distraction for UC Irvine, according to the "I Done This" blog, states, "It takes an average of about 25 minutes (23 minutes and 15 seconds exactly) to return to the original task after a distraction."[33] So, a thirty-second disruption, like checking social media, is twenty-five minutes and thirty seconds of interruption. What are some tips and tricks that you can do to avoid this? Plan times to check email and social media at certain points of the day and stick to them. Put your phone on Do not Disturb so that you are not interrupted. I listen to classical music on headphones while working at my day job to get into the zone and keep more on task. Hearing other people's music or conversations can be very disruptive for me.

Don't Multitask: The father of management consulting and best-selling author Peter Drucker, in his seminal book *The Effective Executive*, warns that, "There was Mozart, of course. He could, it seems, work on several compositions at the same time, all of them masterpieces. But he is the only known exception. The other prolific composers of the first rank—Bach, Handel, Haydn, or Verdi—composed one work at a time. They did not begin the next until they finished the preceding one, or until they stopped work on it for the time being and put it away in the drawer."[34] In other words, don't assume you are Mozart. Create a priority list for yourself, and put the work that has the most value at the top of your list and work your way down, delegating, as indicated earlier, low-value work to others when you can. The old phrase, "He can't walk and chew gum at the same time" rings true. Walk or chew gum. That is all.

Boundaries are not just important for work but for life in general, especially with family, friends, and significant others. For those of you who have not established good ones, you will need to start immediately. Wanting to pursue your dreams means sometimes you will have to say no to some social activities and miss some events. You will need to block out time for yourself when you cannot be reached, which means some

33 Blake Thorne, "I Done This, How Distractions At Work Take Up More Time Than You Think" Feb. 2020 http://blog.idonethis.com/distractions-at-work/.

34 Gianna Cary, "The Secret to Productivity is Not a Secret" https://medium.com/agilent-careers/the-secret-to-productivity-is-not-a-secret-60f5978ad302.

people will have to schedule time with you. For the disorganized, messy people in your life, this might cause friction. But as they start to get used to it, they can adapt, learn, and grow, and many will start to respect you and your time. Remember, time is a precious resource, a scarce commodity. It is also finite. Therefore, if it is not working for you, it is working against you. Managing time and setting boundaries is not something you will master right away; like anything else, it is a muscle that needs to be exercised to be strengthened and it will take time and practice to master properly.

Watch YOUR Bottom Line

In business, you must understand your bottom line, which means focusing on the numbers and things that really matter. You only have so much free time to allocate to personal projects, so you must make them count. People often use the phrase "spend time," but we need to have a paradigm shift in understanding to change this phrase to "invest time" instead. You can only invest so much time into your day gig. Why is this? Because at the end of the day, you are not the owner. And for those of you who happen to read this and are the owner either of a business or self-employed (which is also a business, BTW), but it is not fulfilling you, then this counts for you too. The bottom line question to ask is, "Am I staying in the black (profitable) with my investment of time in myself, or am I in the red (negative or lacking) in investing in myself and the projects that matter most to me?"

The businesses you work for are most certainly watching their bottom line and understanding their financial health to see if they can meet all their projections, commitments, and obligations. Are you doing the same? If not, why not? What do you see yourself doing in the next three, six, nine, and twelve months? What are you committed or obligated to do for yourself? Right now I am embarking on releasing a new podcast. We have just finished ten episodes for season one; it is all set up to be released. It has been such a rewarding project, especially being able to do it all remotely.

It has taken a lot of work, time, and money to be able to make the podcast happen, but I have learned so much in the process: scheduling and conducting all of the interviews, finding the software to record, sending all the files to the editor, creating the graphic design, uploading and scheduling for distribution. The key learnings are invaluable, not to mention all the connections I have made. It started as an experiment, to see if I could do it. It turns out I have stumbled upon what I think is a key position and formula, interviewing musicians and engineers about their journey and process from another fellow musician, me! *Deeper Grooves: Musicians on Music* podcast was birthed from a small idea that became a fully realized dream.

If I had waited for the perfect timing, the right opportunity, for a state-of-the-art studio, and an assistant to schedule guests, it would have never happened. The barriers to entry to create these types of projects are low now, and even working with the editor was affordable and enjoyable. I realized by listening to all these artists that everyone has a story to share, so much so that we are already gearing up to start recording season two! By knowing my bottom line I was able to manage my time more efficiently to get this project done.

What is your bottom line? When you get to the end of this year and look back on all your accomplishments, will you have a long list or a short list? Will you be satisfied with what you have done? Will you have gotten that promotion, started that personal project, learned a new skill, gone on that dream vacation, bought that house, climbed that mountain, or volunteered to help humanity? Or will you have spent another year filled with failed new year's resolutions and things that never came to full fruition, things left half done or never started because of fear, lack of time, and commitment, or some other obstacle that was not overcome?

Rudyard Kipling so eloquently said, "*We have forty million reasons for failure, but not a single excuse.*" The only reason we fail at putting ourselves and our projects as a priority in our lives and do not accomplish as much or get things done is that we forget who we are working for—ourselves. You can work for a company and give your blood, sweat, and tears, then be let go during layoffs and replaced by someone faster, better, smarter, and cheaper! Companies have forty million reasons too.

Whether you work your day gig for a short time and have a long-term goal to progress, if your reason for living is not that job, then, yes, it needs to represent one slice of your life pie but not the entire thing.

If you're going to work like a slave, who will be your master? Better it be you than anyone else. You need to learn to master your own dreams, your own desires, and your own destiny. No one else can do it for you. Not your boss, not your mother or father, sister or brother, your significant other, best friend, or anybody else but you.

You cannot let anything come between you and your bottom line. Anyone who tells you that it's not about numbers, it's not about what you produce in the marketplace, is a person who is not going to amount to much. They have no goals, no strategy, but I am sure they have a whole lot of excuses and reasons for living a meaningless, mediocre life. These are people you do not have time for. You can't soar with eagles if you are hanging with turkeys.

I have a friend right now going through a divorce. He spent so much time working on himself and personal development while his wife did not, and eventually they grew apart. Life has a natural way of weeding people out who are not there to support you and your goals. You might be experiencing something similar. Do you find yourself spending more time working on your stuff and unable to hang out with friends, go to parties, or be in relationships with people who are going nowhere? You are going somewhere, and the only way others can go with you is to walk together in the same direction. You must focus on your bottom line, and they should focus on theirs.

If you are in a relationship with a significant other, you will have your goals and they will have theirs. You will also share common goals. If you look at it as a Venn diagram, you have the two circles representing you and your partner, and you can see how much you overlap. To have an effective relationship, there must be some overlap. If you are just too separate circles, you are in trouble. If you have 100 percent overlap, you might have lost yourself in the other person and do not have enough independence, commonly known as codependence.

Relationships, like everything else we have spoken about, require balance. So while you focus on your bottom line, assess the time you can allocate to your individual goals as well as your common goals. If you don't, you could end up getting to the top of the mountain only to realize you are alone and your significant other is far behind you. Sometimes that is for the best, but sometimes you inadvertently did that and must go back to fix that relationship, if it can be salvaged. To summarize, you have several bottom lines for your goals and commitments; in the same way a business would review all of its segments to see the total bottom line, you will have to do so as well.

Your Business Is Your Business

You must sometimes be careful whom you tell your goals to. When you are in the incubation phase, or the early stages, sometimes it is beneficial to tell everyone what you are doing, and sometimes you're better off keeping it to yourself. When Sara Blakely, the billionaire inventor of Spanx®, was making her prototypes in her early days, she spent over a year in research and development working on her own before ever telling friends or family members about her venture.

Why do you think she did that? Sometimes your family, wanting what's best for you, doesn't want to see you struggle or lose everything, and that can sometimes discourage you from trying something new. What if you look foolish? What if no one likes it? What if you lose your shirt?! You already have the fear monster inside you telling you these things, and you don't want to amplify it by having others saying what you are already worried about. Plus, you don't want their judgment. I believe they have the best intentions, but sometimes they can distract and dissuade us from doing what we need to do on our own. Zig Ziglar (paraphrased) explains, "You share your *give-up goals* with everyone.

But you share your *go-up goals* with a select few." What are give-up goals, though? Give-up goals are things like, "I am going to give up eating ice cream or watching TV." These are goals you tell everyone so that they can encourage you and keep you accountable. Go-up goals state, "I want to become a lawyer," or "I am going to write a book." You might tell only a select few, an inner circle, who can encourage and keep you accountable, but not people who will tell you not to do it. Ziglar also warns, "Don't let someone who gave up on their dreams talk you out of going after yours."

Your business is also your responsibility. If it goes belly up, or something important does not get done, it is 100 percent on you. If you set a goal and do not complete it, you will only have yourself to blame.

For those of you not focusing on a "business" but more of a personal goal, it still rings true. If you don't lose that weight, if you don't start that podcast, if you don't write down those recipes, it will never happen. Only you can do it.

Your day gig is always focusing on itself by default. Your employers may care deeply for you as an employee, but only to the point that you produce and add value to the company. If you could by incapacitation or disability no longer perform your job, they would not keep you on indefinitely and/or they might have to let you go. In the same way, if something is deterring you or keeping you from realizing your full potential, you will have to let it go.

The philosopher Epictetus said it best: "*Keep your attention focused entirely on what is truly your own concern and be clear that what belongs to others is their business and none of yours.*" Knowing what your business is, and what their business is, is the utmost priority. So often we are pondering about what others have and minding their business when we should be minding and mining our own. If you drive a car looking at what is happening in the other cars, and not paying attention to what is happening right in front of you, you will crash.

As a musician, it is exceedingly difficult to not look around, not compare. I was so proud of my 300,000 streams on Spotify, then I saw another artist post about his ten million streams. But since I have been working hard on myself, I realized that his success does not take away or add to my own. I can be happy for him, knowing that he put in the hard work to get to where he is; on a smaller scale, I put in the same hard work to get where I am. My being upset at him would not add one more stream to my numbers, and why would I want to take away from this person anyway? Psychologists warn us to avoid "compared despair," thus saving us from unwanted depression and jealousy in the process.

Often people have a poor mentality, which states, "I don't have anything, so I'll steal from someone else in order to have it." That is only a temporary solution. You will always be looking over your shoulder, for one, but also you will know you didn't work to get it, so you won't feel that great about your accomplishment or lack thereof. Depression starts when you covet what others have. Others have their own dreams, and you must have yours. "God bless the child that's got his own," right?

Now What?

So now that you have your own business in mind, what are you going to do to shape it, nurture it, and help it to grow? Knowing and doing are not the same thing. *Where* you have the knowledge also is important. There is head knowledge and there is heart/gut knowledge. The former will only get you so far, but the latter packs a punch. Your business approach must involve a good mix of both types of knowledge to succeed. It cannot be all head or all heart. It requires balance.

It all goes back to the theory of You, Inc. Everything is up to *you*. You have no one else to blame, and you must get up every day and sacrifice to make it happen. You must try harder than you have ever tried. You must keep yourself accountable and motivated even when it seems hopeless and the excitement has dwindled. There will be many times when you will want to quit. It will be challenging but rewarding. You must celebrate small wins. You must know when to ask for help. You must manage your own self-care. It's a lot. Therefore, many don't succeed. If it were easy everyone would be doing it. Everyone would be balling right now (some are bawling right now as they read this). You have to do it all, as your own Superman or Superwoman, but I know you can do it. And I believe in you.

Your Boss Does Not Care About You

I know this sounds harsh, but it is true. The only one who cares if you succeed is you. Your boss is focused on his or her success and only cares about your success up to the point it coincides with theirs. Some of you will have great success at work, but many of you reading this will find your life's fulfillment outside of your nine-to-five. In either case, freeing yourself from the idea that your boss or company is responsible for your success will help to put you on the right track.

Businesses are not altruistic unless they are nonprofit charities. Most of our day gigs are places where they would easily replace us with someone else if the opportunity arose. Why? Are we so easily replaceable? Oftentimes, yes. I know that hurts your feelings, but it is true. Sometimes it is good for both companies and us to be replaced. I have been let go or fired from a few positions in my day and it always freed me to find a better opportunity in the long run.

How many of you have stayed much longer than you should have in relationships, jobs, or other situations that you knew weren't great for you? Many things in life have an expiration date, and just like milk that has gone bad, the longer you stay, the more it stinks. But some of us must be forcibly pushed out of a situation before we move or act. We are creatures of habit and fall into complacency. Because routines make it easy to fall into a pattern, day in and day out.

And think about it. How often does your boss ask you how you are doing? How are you feeling? Is there anything they can do to help you succeed? Some dynamic leaders will be more empathetic and will ask these questions, but many will not because they are so caught up in their own bubble of worry, anxiety, work problems, and other things.

It does not make your boss a bad person for not asking; it means you must become an employee who is not looking for validation or affirmation at work. If you have this at work, it is icing on the cake; but for those of you who don't, it is okay. You will become stronger being more self-reliant and self-affirming. What you should learn to do is be more proactive and bring more of your skills you are honing outside of the job into your work, if possible.

Bring Your Side Hustle To Work Day

In my personal life, I started making video content for my music. Because of that, I started to not only learn the craft of how to make award-winning videos, but to assemble a team, tell a compelling story, and distribute this content via various channels. So when I took over content creation at work, it was easy for me to draw on those skills—to bring in outside editors and photographers and work with in-house graphic designers to create the content that we needed.

For you it may not be as simple, but you can start to think about things you are doing outside of work that you could incorporate, then let your boss know you have these skills. I knew of a person who in their personal time studied mindfulness; she eventually brought meditation and yoga into her office job. I remember another person who made baked goods at home who was tapped to make several cakes for office birthdays; and yet another retail store coworker who made macaroons for our store events! You will have to think outside of the box, which is not a bad thing, but it might be worth letting your boss in on the secret that you have other skills that might be useful to the firm, if given a chance or opportunity. You never know until you try, and they will never know until you speak up.

Don't Assume

Often, we assume that our bosses can read our minds, but you must be forthright and tell them. In a passive-aggressive world, many of us hold a lot back, at work and in relationships. I cannot tell you how many times I have had exes who were mad at me for something and then later would say, "You should have known," but they never told me to my face what was bothering them. Your boss will be astonished when you tell them of these skills you possess that they never knew existed.

They need you to communicate, and in a perfect world they would also tell you what you need to know. But good communication can be severely lacking in the corporate environment, and, when working in a smaller setting, it can be even harder, not because of office politics but because of how small the team is. There might not be much of a buffer between you and them.

To conclude, some bosses and companies are great to their employees. I have worked for bosses who have mentored me and helped me chart out my success. But even then, I always have worked on my music outside of my day job. I do not foresee that ever changing. I believe you must be diversified, and you need passion projects, side hustles, and hobbies to stay sane. Many of us who do not have this feel more burnt out and do not have the proper outlets to express themselves openly.

It is not ultimately your boss's responsibility to shape and mold your career. It would be nice if they took the time to do so, but many will not for various reasons. If you want that promotion, you are going to have to ask for it and work for it. It will not just fall into your lap. You must gain the necessary skills, create the plan, and attack it with a vengeance. You must take your work to the next level. You have to make your boss, your team, and your company take notice. And if they don't or won't, as mentioned earlier, then you might need to consider taking your skills to a new firm or starting your own thing where you will be appreciated and utilized to your full capacity, and compensated for all the time you spent increasing your value through personal development.

Focusing On Yourself Is Selfless, Not Selfish

If you remember nothing else from this chapter, remember that focusing on yourself is one of the most empowering and beneficial things that you can do. Some people will struggle with this concept because they feel it is selfish. It seems counterintuitive, but if you think about it, it makes perfect sense. In the classic scenario of being on an airplane, in the event of an emergency you have to put your oxygen mask on before you help anyone else. Why is this? Because if you pass out, you will not be able to help yourself or anyone else, then you become dead weight, or a liability to everyone around you.

Think of another example. In the Bible, the Good Samaritan was only able to help the poor man who had been beaten, robbed, and left for dead on the side of the road because he had money. He was able to put the man on his camel, take him to a nearby inn, and leave silver coins to pay for his care, and an IOU basically stating if anything was owed on the balance, he would pay it on his next trip to that town. If the Good Samaritan had been broke, down on his luck, or also just beaten and robbed, he would have been no help to this poor, defenseless man.

For years I used to forsake my own health. I would crisscross the entire city to run after everyone and stayed out late drinking a lot, until one day my body just gave out. I could have blamed everyone, but in the end I only had myself to blame. I had done it to my own body because I was not well versed in the art of self-care and self-love.

Love Yourself First

Now I spend my days making sure I take my medications. I have been clean and sober eight months, getting my ten thousand steps a day walking around the neighborhood, and I meditate often. I also take time to work on my personal projects. I am incorporating more fresh produce into my diet. I also read and listen to book summaries, podcasts, and watch documentaries to edify my mind, body, soul, and spirit.

I learned from transformation guru Lisa Nichols to give out of my abundance, not my lack. She calls it giving from your saucer, not your cup. Essentially, if you fill a tea cup on a saucer with liquid and let it overflow, you are supposed to keep your tea cup (which is you and your needs) always full and then give out of the overflow, whatever lands in the saucer. Doing all these self-care routines are filling my cup, and I find that I am so fulfilled now, I can finally give to others.

I have been able to lend money, invest in projects, and donate my time and energy to helping others' dreams come true. I have mentored and taught people in goal setting, financial literacy, and the craft of making music. It has been immensely rewarding as I can look back at all the lives I have influenced and helped, and that makes me feel good.

I never would have been able to do any of that if I had let myself go. If I was tired, depressed, lethargic, sickly, and spent no time building myself up in my own personal development and completing my own projects and gaining new skills, I could not be a good mentor or role model.

Self-Care Is

Sometimes we do not understand what self-care and self-love is. I like taking baths, listening to classical music or jazz, taking walks, chatting with friends, making music for fun, and learning/reading. All of those are acts of love and self-care for me. Nourishing the body, mind, and soul is not only beneficial but crucial to staying in tip top shape and performance.

Some people may think they do not have the time, with all their current demands, or don't know how to do this because they are stuck thinking about "someday," which never comes. Some people think self-care is stupid, and that they should push themselves to the brink of breaking, that they are big and tough and strong and they can take it, as if taking time for yourself is a sign of weakness. It is a position of strength, knowing that you are doing what is best for you. I see it a lot in women, especially moms who will do everything for their families but then stop getting their hair and nails done, or stop taking time to chat with girlfriends, or just basically run themselves into the ground only to then take it out on their spouses and children. I have seen it equally in men who work extra hours and go help people move and do yard work and whatever other "man duties" they can around the house to be helpful, but they neglect their family or health in the process and end up getting really sick or make poor decisions.

Stop Suffering

A good friend of mine, author Blake Bauer, when discussing thoughts from his book *You Were Not Born to Suffer*, in an article for *Soul & Spirit* magazine on self-love and self-care, explains four keys to love. He believes that to love yourself *today*, you must learn to express your true feelings, act in alignment (be true to yourself), make space for *you*, and take care of *your* mind. He says, "The belief that loving and valuing yourself is a negative expression of selfishness is completely false."

Like anything else, you must decide if it is selfless (positive) or selfish (negative). The power of saying no is especially important to self-care and self-love as well. Saying no to things that are not good for you or not valuable or do not bring you joy is a good thing. Sometimes you have to say no to being around certain people who bring you down or discourage you from doing what is right for you, and that might be difficult but it's necessary. You must choose to say what you need to say, kindly, but be firm. You may have to say, "When you act like this, I cannot be around you. When you are drinking and smoking around me, that is not a good, healthy environment for me to be in. It does not align with my new values or goals." You may have to say, "I cannot attend that event. I am working on a personal project," or "I cannot come help you with that thing you needed because I have already overcommitted myself this week and need to create some space and down time for me today." Similarly, you have to create new habits to fulfill your self-care goals. Let's say the alarm is blaring and you do not want to get up, but you've decided you need to wake up ten to fifteen minutes earlier so that you have time to meditate and get your mind in a conducive state to be its best today. You have to say no to the part of you that wants to hit snooze, and get up to do what is good for your mental health and self-care/self-love.

I really like how Blake ends the article, stating, "You are finally taking care of the miracle that is your life. It's time to stop betraying yourself, because you're the one you've been waiting for. You are the love you have been seeking." How many of us need to awaken to the thought that we are living, breathing miracles? That we need to finally start taking better care of these vessels that we have been gifted. That we have been betraying and sabotaging ourselves for years, and it is time that we put a stop to it. We have often spent too much time focusing on the external when we need to be focused on the internal. You need to operate out of love for yourself first, and then let that permeate out to the rest of the world—to your sphere of influence and those you care for and love the most. Then, and only then, can you come from a place of abundance to serve and to give, instead of a place of anxiety, worry, frustration, and lack. Work on and take care of yourself, and the rest will all fall into place.

Answer These Questions:

1. Even if you work for an employer, how can you see yourself as self-employed?
2. What can you do to manage your self-care?
3. What inner work do you need to do to love yourself more?

9.

Finding A Work/Life Balance

> *"We need to do a better job of putting ourselves higher on our own 'to do' list."* —Michelle Obama, former First Lady

My girlfriend sent me an article from a few years ago in *Harvard Business Review* by author Kabir Sehgal explaining why you should have more than one career. "*It's not uncommon to meet a lawyer who'd like to work in renewable energy, or an app developer who'd like to write a novel, or an editor who fantasizes about becoming a landscape designer*," says Sehgal. In fact, Seghal has four vocations: corporate strategist, U.S. Navy reservist, author, and record producer. I have a few vocations and hobbies myself: head of digital for a global beauty company, music artist, music publisher, producer, label owner, author, podcast host, and public speaker. I think we should all have many vocations *and* many hobbies.

As mentioned earlier, being involved in Toastmasters has tremendously helped me in all my vocations and is a great educational hobby for me. Warren Buffet sings the praises of similar training programs that teach public-speaking skills, which he says help for a lifetime. Not only has it proven to be an incredibly supportive and nurturing environment for me, it also allows me a safe space to practice and receive valuable feedback. It has also allowed me speaking opportunities and competitions in and outside of the club to sharpen my skills, which I use in my personal life and work.

Toastmasters checks a lot of boxes for me because I love to continually learn new things. It is a fraternal organization where I am able to make friends and network. I even have created a Mastermind (peer to peer mentoring) group from it to discuss strategy and provide encouragement and accountability. I have held several leadership roles during my six years, both in my home club and at the district level, and I have mentored newbies.

I recently had a musician friend who was unable to perform her music after having brain surgery. She got involved in another Toastmasters Club, thus still getting to "perform," just in a different medium. And because of her ordeal, she now has an outlet to share her experiences as well.

You, too, have a story to share and need an outlet. Toastmasters or other public-speaking programs might not be the forum for you, but there are so many other sites and avenues to be able to connect, express yourself, and have fun in positive, more creative ways. I feel sorry for those who have no outlet and no purpose, who might be stuck in dead-end jobs. No wonder people are so resentful, regretful, bitter, and, sometimes, even suicidal. If you do not let it out, you will eventually burst.

Since Toastmasters is mostly known for its public speaking aspects, let me explain a little more about its leadership aspects and how you may be able to find more leadership opportunities in your life. First, leaders are made, they are not born. To learn to lead, you must first follow, then volunteer for more responsibility. Since Toastmasters is a nonprofit, most of the workers are volunteers except for some employees at the corporate headquarters. For many people, including myself, I was able to get leadership opportunities in Toastmasters before I started getting them in my paid job. You may want to find a volunteer organization not only for a chance to give back and for the good feelings the service brings, but also to seek out more leadership opportunities if you don't have them at work or elsewhere. I use every opportunity I can to gain new skills. Maybe that is the super nerd inside of me. You might want to volunteer at a soup kitchen, food bank, literacy program, homeless shelter, or multitudes of places that would welcome people to help, as it would benefit the organization and you.

Exploring hobbies or other activities outside of your day job can provide balance too. People join book clubs; or get into fitness programs, go to the gym, participate in sporting intramurals; or they cook, write, play video games, and so on. The operative word is balance.

You should not work too much or play too much. And for all those who say they don't have the time, like anything else, you will have to make the time. In Los Angeles, everyone talks about how busy they are like it's a badge of honor, but people unbusy themselves for what they want to do. You must find the time and make the time by utilizing your downtime constructively.

Things You Can Do In Your Downtime:

Listen To Audiobooks

Zig Ziglar would always refer to his car as an automobile university and would preach the value of making those long car rides, commuting to and from work, more useful. In a Volpe study, American drivers (on average) spend just under an hour driving every day. The average audiobook is ten hours long. So, in one year you could listen to thirty-six books easily. I once read that most CEOS read about five books per month or sixty books a year, so automobile university would get you halfway there. If books are not your thing, maybe you would fare better with podcasts.

Subscribe To Podcasts

Now that I have started two podcasts, I know that creating them has never been easier with the myriad of simple and free or affordable apps available to help to create and disseminate your ideas. For those who are not prepared to host their own show, you are in luck; we need listeners as well. There are podcasts on every single subject that you can imagine, and several you have never even heard of, but all fascinating. Not all the material is good, so you must sift through the white noise, but cream rises to the top. From motivational speakers and gurus to entertainment and celebrities to titans of industry, spirituality, and much more, it is extremely easy to listen to these audio documentaries on the go.

Watch Documentaries

Living in L.A. so close to Hollywood, the Sony Studios are just a stone's throw from my apartment. Besides the big box entertainment, Netflix and many other outlets have spurred a resurgence of documentaries. I lean heavily into music documentaries, musicals, and concerts, so that is what I mostly watch. Most recently a lot of true crime shows and unsolved mysteries have become binge-worthy, as well as motivational and educational topics. Whatever your choice, just like it is good to swap in healthier snacks to replace junk food, sometimes it is good to switch to some edutainment with your entertainment occasionally.

Take Webinars

Every day in our post-COVID world, I am inundated with invitations to someone's webinar on Zoom, Facebook Live, or YouTube. Recently, I attended a weeklong Facebook Live Comeback Challenge by motivational speaker and author Tony Robbins. Not only was it offered for free (there was a paid Zoom VIP option as well), but he also donated twenty free meals to charity on our behalf just for signing up. The content was available live and on replay for over a week and, yes, I know what you are thinking, what are they selling you at the end? Yes, they did offer a paid experience at the end, but that did not devalue all the great free content from Tony and a team of experts on a variety of subjects, as well as all the camaraderie the participants experienced in the chat bubble. Even if people are trying to sell me something, I still sign up for free experiences to see what they have to say. If you look at every opportunity as a learning experience, it can be the same for you too.

Consume Actual Books

I mentioned audiobooks in this section, but I still love hard copies, just like I listen to music on Spotify but still buy vinyl. We all need options. As a good friend put it, there are formats and then there are experiences. Each experience and the way you consume is different. There is no right or wrong way, but sometimes I find a hard-copy book can make me focus much more, the same as a record makes me listen to an entire album rather than just a few songs.

Peruse Magazines

In 1999, when I started college at Berklee, I begged my mom to buy me a subscription to *Rolling Stone*, which I idolized growing up in the '90s as the holy grail of magazines for music. If you were mentioned in there, or better yet graced the cover, you were not only cool, but popular in the world of entertainment. Fast forward to a few years later, I received a notification that if I paid fifty dollars, I could receive the next fifty years free, and so I mailed a check and I think I now have *Rolling Stone* until the year 2053! I still get it and still read the reviews, but I am not as fanatical as I was in my teens and early twenties. In the last four years, I have also had a subscription to *Success* magazine, which is the only magazine I have ever subscribed to where every article was good, no fluff pieces, and each one is thoroughly enjoyable. If you are not one for reading books, magazines might be a good way to get your reading in quick-bites, especially for those commuting on public transit or Uber.

Go To Concerts

Not just because I am a musician, but because I am a music lover. I spend most of my downtime listening to new music. One way I have discovered new music is by going to concerts. In a post-COVID world, but many artists, including myself, have been flooding social media to connect with our audiences.

Most recently, I attended Live from Our Living Rooms "Creative Summit," where I got to watch very intimate concerts at home by Gretchen Parlato, Terri Lynne Carrington, and Kurt Rosenwinkel. *Relix* magazine has been pushing out more live content by Marcus King Band, and I have seen a lot of concerts by Jam in the Van and Tedeschi Trucks Band as well during this time.

Whether you like classical, jazz, funk, or classic rock, there is a station and a live concert happening somewhere, just waiting for you. It is especially important that while you try to maintain all your work and personal projects that you allow yourself some downtime, to recharge and recuperate. Whatever works for you. Luckily, I picked a vocation like music, which is fun and exciting, and can be my vocation and my relaxation. But for everyone, I cannot see a downside to seeing concerts.

What was the last great concert you have watched? What do you love most about watching music? I think oftentimes we become so busy we forgo things that we like because we become too serious about life. The old saying "All work and no play makes Jack a dull boy" is true. Psychologist Mihalyi Csikszentmihalyi said, "*Once we realise that the boundaries between work and play are artificial, we can take matters in hand and begin the difficult task of making life more livable.*" This is an important distinction—that life becomes more livable from having work/life balance; but the balance comes from not knowing where one stops and one starts—to inject fun into both work and play, create space and time for both, and have an equal balance of time spent doing what you love.

Practicing Mindfulness And Harmony

Being at a concert is made much better if you practice mindfulness, which is a struggle for me. I struggle to focus and be present in the moment. It is fun to watch a concert happening live, in real time. Watching it on demand later is fun but not as fun as the live experience. Knowing that someone is doing it as you are watching is what "live" is all about. There are no do-overs; it is whatever it will be.

So everything has a balance. I have the balance not only between my day gig and my side projects but also in music, being the performer and creator and being a supporter, listener, and spectator. When I start to feel the friction in my life, it is when something is out of balance.

Music in and of itself is balance. That is harmony. And thus, when you are watching a concert, whether alone or with friends, you, too, should be in harmony. You should not be at the concert thinking about work. But it is not always easy. Sometimes I answer emails while at the concert, sometimes I send texts, sometimes I take pictures or videos or post online or look at social media—thus I'm not fully experiencing it. To have paid all this money to see someone only to have never really seen them and enjoyed myself as much as I could is a waste.

My best suggestion is to turn off the phone. It is okay to unplug and not be reachable for a moment. Isn't it better to be social with friends at the concert who are with you, or just be with the band you are watching, than to be so easily distracted by things that are most likely not very important in the grand scheme of things? Why do we do this? Are we that starved for constant connection? Do we really fear missing out on something else that much? I think we are, and I think we do, through bad conditioning. We must reprogram ourselves to be more present in the moment, letting go of distractions. It is a fact that many people cannot sleep as well because of light and noise pollution and that they stare at screens so much before bed that it throws off their sleep rhythms. Watch the concert, enjoy, and forget about work. Press Play and relax a bit. You've earned it. Part of the balance is being mindful enough to know you took time off from work, otherwise you will feel like you are always in work mode.

Binge Watch Content

The term "Netflix and chill" has become a phrase of our times. We coin phrases that fit our current lifestyle and would have sounded foreign even twenty years ago. Nowadays I chuckle at the use of the eggplant emoji because it doesn't stand for an eggplant anymore. I used to believe that watching TV was a waste of time and purposely avoided getting sucked into shows that become time vampires, sucking up all my free time (like I have any). But living through the post-COVID world, I have found binge watching to not only be therapeutic but also a necessary evil. I have always loved documentaries, and Netflix, Amazon Prime, HBO Max, and other platforms offer lots of really good ones. But even if you decide to watch the latest *Housewives*, or *Masked Singer*, or whatever reality TV show, singing competition, or tween drama that floats your boat, I think this is a very healthy, happy way to wind down.

For years I have been laser focused on productivity, like a juicer trying to squeeze every ounce of creative juice from my lifeless pulp of a body, to maximize all of my time, only to have cycles of burnout, depression, and utter exhaustion. It is very tiring. You hit a wall and the law of diminishing returns starts to slowly creep in. You come to a point where your brain is mush and you are devoid of coherent thoughts. I call this the Blue Light Zone.

This is the time to lie in bed or on the couch and veg out to the latest and greatest in content. And there is no shortage of content. Every week there is a new app, a new show, a new season of something coming out, for your viewing pleasure. What better way to incorporate work/life balance than to carve out a few hours to enjoy the best and worst of what the Media has to offer?

Again, the key is balance. You cannot watch so much TV that you don't get the most important things done. You cannot watch TV when you are supposed to be working, cleaning, or doing your personal projects. Too much exposure to blue light can keep you up late, too, so you have to watch out for that, but in moderation it can be enjoyable and beneficial.

How Much Free Time Do We Actually Have?

Many of us have more free time than we think, but some of us are using it to watch too much television. A week has 168 hours and we spend about forty hours working. We spend fifty-six hours sleeping, which leaves seventy-two hours. With that many hours, excluding other commitments, how much TV does the average American watch per week? According to A.C. Nielsen Co., the average American watches four hours of TV/day, twenty-eight hours a week, or two months of nonstop TV watching per year! This can be a particularly good or an unbelievably bad thing. Like anything else, it is all about balance and intentionality.

As aforementioned, I try to balance my TV time with edutainment and entertainment to avoid becoming a rotten couch potato. I also try to watch TV only after everything else is done for the day with work or personal projects, or when my mind, body, and spirit is saying, "You have done all you can do today." I get all my chores, errands, exercise, cooking, and other stuff done. I listen to classical music while I work and meditate either in the morning or at night, so I have that covered. But I struggle sometimes thinking I could do something else with that time instead of watching TV. There is nothing my girlfriend and I like more than curling up and watching TV, but we also try to fit in our walks and other activities, so when we do watch TV, it is intentional. Often, we'll have dinner at the table, listening to music or talking, then watch TV as a "dessert" treat.

There is a school of thought comparing free time and invested time. Some of you are not investing time in yourself so you do not have free time to spare; instead, you have opportunity cost time, losing out on precious opportunities by not earmarking time for what is most important for you to succeed in life. If you could watch one less hour of TV per day, cutting down to three, and use that time to acquire a new skill or read, join a study group, or work on something you have been putting off, you would feel better about yourself and get more done.

So it is not a question of "Should I do something productive, or should I watch TV?" it is more of a question of "Did I do something productive, and can I reward myself with TV instead?" If you work yourself to death, you will be stressed and burnt out; if you watch endless amounts of TV, you won't get enough done. There is a work/life balance, and there is a free time/invested time balance too.

As William Feather is quoted as saying, "We all find time to do what we really want to do." Be more mindful in your approach to playtime. When you are about to Netflix and Chill, take a self-inventory of your day and decide if you have unlocked that reward based on the actions and intentions you took, and put a cap on how much you watch. But if you know in your heart of hearts you have been killing it at work and your side hustle and you need to blow off steam so you can get back up and go back out there and slay more dragons tomorrow, put your feet up and enjoy binging!

The Importance Of Family Time

My mom and sister make fun of me because they know I try to schedule my calls with them. In fact, last weekend I scheduled a FaceTime call with my mom to meet her new boyfriend. I do this because I usually have such a jam-packed schedule that I am always doing something or with someone and have to text, "Can't talk right now." Thus, I feel the stress of wanting to talk to them but must wrestle with the inner conflict of other priorities and commitments, or lacking privacy or a moment to myself. It can be very frustrating for a planner like me to have constant intrusions, and nothing can feel more intrusive than an unscheduled phone call, even from someone you want to speak with, not just annoying bill collectors and salespeople.

But as I've gotten older, I've realized that not everything can be scheduled and not everyone is a by-the-clock type of person, so I must relax and allow grace to speak to friends and family on their timetable, which is not always synched to mine. At the end of my life, I am sure that I am not going to be wishing more people scheduled more calls with me. I'll regret not answering those intrusive calls when I had the chance, especially if those people are no longer with me.

Out of all the work/life balancing acts you must do, and all the balls in the air, if you must drop one, drop work before you drop friends or family. When you are having a hard time in life, work is not going to come and sit with you at two a.m. and talk about it, or hold you while you are crying, or tell you that it is going to get better. I remember my youngest uncle on my dad's side, who unfortunately passed over fifteen years ago. I still hear his voice over the phone saying, "Beverly Hills [that's what he called me because what showed up on caller ID], when are you coming to visit me?" He lived in Georgia, and I was just about to go on my first Euro trip, so I told him, "As soon as I get back from my trip, I will start planning to make a visit." I was gone for twenty-one days with two friends, backpacking through Europe with little access to email or phone, but when I landed back in the States, I had several messages from family telling me that my favorite uncle had passed away at age thirty-three. So the visit to Georgia for the funeral was not the visit I had wanted to plan. I learned from that day on not to put off visiting someone or doing something, because tomorrow is not promised to any of us. I regret not going sooner.

In April 2017, I had just gotten back from a trip to Hawaii for vacation to visit a friend with a friend and a weeklong trip to China for a writing camp with music friends. My great-grandma had been sick for quite some time, and my father also had his fiftieth surprise birthday party coming up, and my sister wanted me to be there. So I decided to make the trip home to the East Coast. I was able to see my great-grandma in the hospital. She was so tired and hooked up to tubes, but she was happy to see me. I remember running around the hospital looking for change to buy her a newspaper. She was asleep by the time I got back, but I left it on her table and told the nurse to let her know I left it for her. That was the last time I spoke to her. She died a month later. But this time I made sure to go, as I knew the end was near.

We do not always have the luxury of knowing the end is coming, which is why we must always live knowing that the end is imminent for all of us—anytime, any day. I am writing this book to help others get more accomplished, but also to remind you to cherish your friends and family. Work will always be there, but these people, including yourself may not.

Again, it is all about life balance. I look back on so many fond memories I have had over the years with friends and family. Facebook is always sending me reminders of the good times and those we have lost along the way. I carry a torch in my heart and soul for those who have passed and work hard to make my dreams come true for them as well as myself. People matter most.

Nurture Your Relationships

When you look at your Wheel of Life, where do friends and family or relationships fall? Are they at the top or bottom of the scale? Is that where you want them to be? Relationships are a lot of work. For me, friends and family are 80 percent, and that is rather good because I do not give anything 100 percent, as I feel there is always room for improvement. My main focus now is mindfulness, really being in the moment, especially with my girlfriend. When I am with friends and family, I'm really thinking about them, not work and other projects. It is so easy to get distracted, which is why meditation is so difficult for me but it's something I must work on and get better at. It is a lifelong practice.

If you have been struggling in this area of work/life balance, don't give up. You can get better. Just like a baby learning to walk, you just must recognize you need to improve and take many baby steps toward that improvement. It will not happen overnight, but it will be extremely rewarding in the end. When you get to the end of your life, you want to be surrounded by friends and family and loved ones. No one wants to be alone.

Make the commitment to take small actions to be a better friend, better companion, and better family member. Maybe you can commit to at least one call a week, making sure to give that person you're speaking with your undivided attention. When you give people all of you, it really makes a huge difference.

The Side Hustler's Side Hustle

Everyone who knows me knows that I have various side hustles, most involving music. In fact, recently a friend said, "I see on Facebook. You are CEO of your own company. Tell me more about that." I replied, "I actually have three companies." Even within those there is always a new venture springing up, like writing this book, or launching two new podcasts. I try to do as much work I love in my non-day-gig work hours, at night and on the weekend. I also spend a considerable amount of time teaching and mentoring to give back. I enjoy the variety.

So why do I think you should have a few more hobbies, personal projects, businesses, and part-time jobs? As Elton John once said in *Rolling Stone*, "If you don't get the music out, you'll go crazy!" I know many people die with the music inside them, and I do not want that to happen to either of us. But for all of you who are already side hustling, why do I think you should add something new periodically to your already overfilled plate? Because we often underestimate what we can do in the long term and overestimate what we can do in the short term. Not everything we plant today will spring up at the same time; thus we need to plant many seeds in order to reap a bountiful harvest later. We also learn exponentially by doing this.

While working on my new *Deeper Grooves* podcast, I have been able to learn how to cold-contact high-profile musicians and schedule shows; how to research, prepare, and conduct interviews; how to record shows, how to create a podcast format and graphics; how to work with an editor; how to post, publish, and distribute to all the major platforms; and how to promote it. And I am sure as I continue to work on it (currently scheduling season 3), I will learn even more. I also have the great feeling you get by having an idea that has come fully to fruition in only a matter of months.

Maybe podcasting is not your thing, but whatever your thing is, I encourage you to step out on faith and make something happen for yourself. My co-host on my *Running Scared* podcast, Brian Sturges, says, "There are doers and there are losers!" A lot of people think I am too harsh when I say that most people make excuses for their lives. I already know many of you are putting off something that you could be doing today and, as Jim Rohn says, "There is always a good excuse but never a good reason."

Learning by doing is a theory espoused by philosopher John Dewey. According to the *Encyclopedia of the Sciences of Learning*, it is "*the process where people make sense of their experiences, especially those experiences in which they actively engage in making things and exploring the world.*" This is commonly called "experiential learning." The ThinkFun Education blog explains the importance of hands-on learning, stating, "Studies have shown that kinesthetic learning or 'doing' helps students to gain a better understanding of the material." It is the preferred method (of the four learning styles, the others being visual, reading/writing, and auditory learning), explaining that students don't always want to be talked to, they want to be taught, and experience is often the best teacher."

Think back to your last school experience. Do you remember what your teacher said compared with group projects you did or field trips you took? I don't remember every music class, but I remember the performances. I don't remember my science lectures, but I remember my science fair project where I treated plants with cancer with beta carotene (vitamin A). I don't remember math tests or my SATS at all. Every time I *do* something, I not only gain a new skill, I gain a longer lasting memory. I usually remember what I learned and how I felt.

What do you want to remember most, as you look back over your life? All the TV shows you watched or all the projects you finished? Maybe you want to remember all the mountains you climbed, trips you took, businesses you built, and songs, movies, books, TV shows, podcasts, and classes you created.

I am an ordinary person who has done extraordinary things simply because I put my mind to it, and you can do it too. You have many skills already that can translate into other areas. It is an investment in yourself, your future, and it will take time, money, resources, energy, and effort but will be rewarding and often lucrative.

My suggestion is to try several things to narrow down what you want to do. Start generating a list of possible side hustles and hobbies. Then start looking at your network to see if there is anyone doing something directly or similarly to what you want to do, and ask them out for coffee or schedule a FaceTime or Zoom meeting to pick their brain on the subject. I have, while working on the podcast, found that people don't mind talking about themselves if you approach it as wanting to learn from them in an informational interview. And speaking to them will most certainly spark even more ideas and help you to know if you are on the right track or need to reevaluate something in your initial plans. Either way, it is another experience moving you slightly closer to your goal of side hustling more.

Hobbies For Non-Side Hustlers

Some of you are not working on side hustles—you just want more time for hobbies, which is great. Whether working on alternative income sources, volunteer work, church, or other hobbies it's important to have something outside of your work that you can focus on to improve and enjoy. I was cursed with a lack of coordination or desire to physically exert myself, thus sports in all forms never appealed to me as a participant or spectator, but I see the benefit in taking up a sport or exercise routine for the pure fun and enjoyment.

I have always been a fan of walking, and now with my goal of ten thousand steps per day, I do it for health, but I also enjoy getting out of my studio apartment and into the urban sprawl (which is as close to nature as I will get). It is low-impact and easy on my body, yet physical enough to get some much-needed cardio. I can throw on my headphones and listen to Spotify and easily walk ninety to one hundred twenty minutes. I know many people in California who enjoy hiking, but I have never been a fan. To each their own.

I used to collect shot glasses (when I used to drink) from all the places I visited, until I had so many I had no more room to fit them on my shelf. Others collect Beanie Babies, art, books, or vinyl records. I know of an elderly gentleman, Joel Forman, who has amassed a huge coin collection and is spending the latter part of his life donating his coins to various museums, including the Smithsonian. In fact, he has given me a vintage copperhead penny and a half dime (not to be confused with a nickel since it's made from silver), which I keep on the shelf under my shot glass collection.

Not only was coin collecting a hobby for Joel, eventually it became a full-time job in retirement as he became a senior accredited and certified numismatic (coins and currency) appraiser with the American Society of Appraisers, where he has been a professional for over thirty years; at eighty years of age now, he has written several articles for *Coin World* magazine.

There is a great article on the blog C&T Publishing (for creative quilting and sewing) explaining "the importance of hobbies" as it relates to reducing stress. Author Maria Cannon states, "*Hobbies play an important role in mitigating some of the unavoidable stress, as they provide us within an outlet for creativity, distraction, and something to look forward to. Hobbies bring a sense of fun and freedom to life that can help minimize the impact of chronic stress.*"[35]

Who doesn't have an overabundance of stress in their lives? Many people lack the creative outlets to channel and harness this stress into more productive and useful activities. Without them, people tend to be angry and snap more easily or turn to alcohol and other substances to help cope. According to spacioustherapy.com, "Chronic stress is the most harmful type of stress. If chronic stress is left untreated over a long period of time, it can significantly and often irreversibly damage your physical health and deteriorate your mental health."[36]

It is impossible to curate and create a life that has zero stress. If having active hobbies can help minimize and help mitigate chronic stress, what keeps you from taking more action to do it? It is likely that you are so stressed you don't know where to begin. Your unchecked, prolonged high level of stress has debilitated you, and you only have enough energy to maintain. This is similar to how people who never exercise when starting up a routine have difficulty fighting through a lifetime of lethargy.

The good news is the cure for both is the same: start small. When Joel was starting his coin collection, he inherited quite a bit from his dad,

35 Maria Cannon, "The Importance of Hobbies," C&T Publishing https://www.ctpub.com/blog/the-importance-of-hobbies/.

36 Shawna Freshwater, "3 Types of Stress and Health Hazards," PhD, Spacious Therapy, https://spacioustherapy.com/3-types-stress-health-hazards/.

but I can imagine he added to it a few coins at a time. We must reprogram our mind to get rid of the all-or-nothing mentality that has been ingrained in us. If we cannot do thirty minutes a day, then we do zero minutes instead. This is both counterproductive and counterintuitive. Even now that I mentor, I say start small and underwhelm yourself so that you know it is easy to stick with. When I sat down to write this book, I broke it into sections. Each section is about three pages, so I wrote three pages at a time, which took about an hour. I knew that I could find at least one hour per day to dedicate to writing if I planned accordingly. Some days I wrote ten to twenty pages over several hours. But if I had said I was going to write five hours a day, knowing I have other projects and other commitments, I would have ended up sabotaging myself. I would have had a few productive days, then something would ultimately have come up, causing me to fail or give up altogether, scrapping the project at the first sign of imperfection.

Hopefully, the hobby or hobbies you pick bring you so much happiness and joy that you find it easy to make time for them. I know that it is not always easy, especially for those who have kids or elderly loved ones who need your time and attention, but you still have to squeeze in some "me time" doing something that helps destress you.

If your hobby is making you more stressed, then you need to reevaluate it. If you are not loving it anymore, it may be time to pick a new one. According to *SWNS Digital*, "We dedicate 245 hours a year to our hobbies."[37] There are an endless amount of hobbies to choose from, with various costs to start. Whole stores and blogs are dedicated to finding them, some that can be done solo or in groups. There is literally something for everyone, at any age or walk of life, at any time. I encourage you to try something new; you may love it and feel better and less stressed after. And if you don't, you can always try, try again, until you do find something you love.

37 "This is how long the average person will stick with a hobby," SWNS Digital Jan. 2019 https://www.swnsdigital.com/2019/01/this-is-how-long-the-average-person-will-stick-with-a-hobby/.

Answer These Questions:

1. How can you start to achieve a better work/life balance?
2. What are some additional hobbies you could take up for fun?
3. How will you find time for them?
4. What do you enjoy doing in your down time?

10.

Learn From The Best

> *"Live as if you were to die tomorrow. Learn as if you were to live forever."* —Mahatma Gandhi, social activist

John Hope Bryant

It is fascinating to read through my old notes and listen to archival interviews I recorded on my iPhone 4 from 2014 when working on *The Art of Awesome*, a book I started but never finished where I interviewed highly successful people to ascertain how they became awesome. I had the pleasure of speaking with John Hope Bryant during the time I was volunteering for his Operation Hope project, a nationwide financial literacy program in the United States. I went to a book signing and he took some time out of his busy schedule to answer some questions from me, a budding author. I'm including some of the key insights here because the information is as poignant and relevant six years later as it was then.

In working over twenty years helping to promote and teach financial literacy to at-risk youth in America, John Hope Bryant spoke about how he overcomes the feeling of helplessness when confronted with daunting tasks: "Developing a concept to change communities from the ground up can be overwhelming, frustrating, fun, and joyful all at the same time," he said. "Now, 20 years later, I have learned that a change can be made with one step."

John Hope Bryant is a remarkable man. And given the current civil unrest, he remains a beacon of light to outshine the darkness in our 2020 political climate and in our underserved communities. The best advice

Bryant ever gave me was that "sometimes your life is the only Bible people will read." That one step for positive change will not only affect you but everyone around you and everyone who comes after you. We are very much monkey see monkey do. Knowing one person can achieve success, making the impossible possible, now seems a reality.

Back in 2014, I stepped out on faith, asking people to allow me to interview them and the most unique thing happened; many of them said yes. I learned there is power in the press, and that being an author can open doors that being a salesman or pitching something just doesn't accomplish.

The beauty of being in America is that you can wake up one day and decide to make a change. I woke up one day, decided to write, and now I am a writer. You can wake up one day, decide to start a business, and you become an entrepreneur. Not every country allows its citizens to do that, and in that I am profoundly grateful to be in the u.s.

You have all the tools inside you, just like Dorothy in *The Wizard of Oz*. She always had the ruby slippers to go home again, but she had to learn to activate them by clicking her heels three times, saying, "There's no place like home." Throughout the Bible there are miracles that happen from something small being multiplied, like feeding the five thousand with two fish and five loaves of bread. You only need to plant one seed to yield a harvest of many fruits.

John Hope Bryant and all the volunteers, including myself, planted seeds of hope and financial literacy because we knew it would be easier for people to "wake up" and make those positive changes, like Dorothy when she was told about it by the Good Witch. Many of you are still waiting for your Good Witch to come along. So let John Hope Bryant and me tell you what you need to know: Start learning the tricks of the trades from the masters before you. Read their lives as your Bible.

A person who is more successful than you has failed more times than you, taken more risks than you, and learned more valuable lessons than you. You may not have the luxury of time or resources, or the capacity to go out and make those million-dollar mistakes, so why not pull up a chair and listen to what these powerful businessmen and thought leaders have to say?

Perseverance And PhDs

Mr. Bryant left me with two very poignant thoughts that I would like to conclude with—one about perseverance and one about PhDs:

> *"To persevere is the best advice I have received. It does not matter where you come from, your beliefs, or economic status, if you persevere and work hard for what you want, your dreams and goals can be achieved," said Bryant. "Whenever I'm feeling stuck, I like to remember a little wisdom from the late President Coolidge: 'Nothing in the world can take the place of persistence. Talent will not; nothing is more common than unsuccessful men with talent. Genius will not; unrewarded genius is almost a proverb. Education will not; the world is full of educated derelicts. Persistence and determination are omnipotent.'"*

Bryant went on to talk about what he calls "The 5 Laws of Love Leadership," summarizing it with one brief statement: "PhDs matter, but 'PhDo's' get the job done."

The whole point of my creating this book, and John Hope Bryant creating Operation Hope, is to inspire the next generation of doers to do something with their lives. The Bible has many chapters, written by many different people. In the same way, we need to see many people doing amazing things in this life and beyond. Those stories need to get passed from generation to generation because those life lessons and morals can still be beneficial many years after death.

If you are looking for an opportunity to learn, the mysteries and secrets of the universe will reveal themselves to you. But, as I have been emphasizing throughout this book, you must seek out knowledge to find knowledge. If you do nothing, you will get nothing. Just like Dorothy clicking her heels, you must do something to get somewhere. It does not just happen on its own; you must create your own magic.

Dr. Ivan Joseph

In 2012, I became obsessed with TED Talks. I have always been a very outward nerd who spent time inside reading books, then graduated to documentaries and eventually speeches. In 2014 as I embarked upon my

TEDX presentation in Napa Valley, I started watching all the best talks, at all levels, offered by a truly diverse group of presenters. One of them happened to be Ivan Joseph, whom I was able to interview about his talk on self-confidence when working on *The Art of Awesome*.

When it comes to the secret sauce for success, self-confidence must rank high up there because I have seen many people who exuded confidence before their success ever came. I always struggled in this area but eventually wrote a song about it called "Confident," which became my biggest hit to date. Dr. Joseph told me, "Without the skill of self-confidence we are useless." The biggest hurdle to self-confidence is negative self-talk, which eats away at any confidence you could have; confidence is a muscle that gets stronger by its repeated use.

Dr. Joseph explains, "We all have this negative self-talk in our heads. Guess what? We have enough people saying we can't do it, we are not good enough. Thoughts influence actions. The more we focus on the negative, we will start believing it. Get away from people who tear you down. We need our own self-affirmations where we tell ourselves, "I am the captain of my ship and the master of my fate."

The latter is a quote from the poet William Ernest Henley and is a mantra that Dr. Joseph has used for many years as a former soccer player and as the head coach for Ryerson University's soccer team, where he oversees a ten million dollar stadium and a hundred million dollar facility. In the description on his TED Talk, "Joseph lists 'self-confidence' as the most underrated and underrepresented skill in his candidates. Fortunately, since he regards it as a skill, he maintains it is something that can be taught. He urges us to transform our negative self-talk (the perpetually negative inner voice telling us we 'can't') into positive self-affirmations like the mantra. Far from being egotistical or having false pride, Joseph firmly considers these moments to be positive reinforcement that attests to who we really are."[38]

38 Vasiliki Marapas, "Self-Confidence as a Skill : skillful self confidence speech," Trendhunter, Nov. 2013 https://www.trendhunter.com/keynote/skillful-self-confidence-speech.

I have since listened to presentations on self-confidence by Brian Tracy, Dale Carnegie, and several others; all the ideas that Dr. Joseph shared with me still ring true in my subsequent study on the subject. It is not something we are necessarily born with, but it is a skill that can be learned; otherwise there would be no reason to write a book about how to improve self-confidence, as no one would be able to change their confidence level from birth.

I do believe that some are naturally more self-confident than others, but a lot of it has to do with environmental feedback. If you always hear, "You can't," or "You're not good enough," then you will often start to operate out of these limiting beliefs. For many of us, we spend a lot of our adult lives on a therapist's couch learning to let go of such limiting beliefs.

If you lack self-confidence, it will be exceedingly difficult for you to speak up for yourself and go after your dreams with abandon. You will always find yourself holding back, which is a shame, because often the quiet person has great ideas but they either don't know it or are too afraid to share them.

I spoke with a female friend in my Masterminds group who told me she finally got the courage to speak up about an issue she was having at work that was not getting resolved, and she felt really upset about it. Now it is being worked on, but nothing would have happened if she hadn't taken action. Being self-confident is understanding your value and your worth, and what you will and will not put up with. A less confident person can often become a doormat, allowing the entire world to walk all over them.

For those of you raising kids, it is important to understand how you can impart more self-confidence into them. Dr. Joseph told me a story about a farmer who would take local boys and have them come work for him. He was known to work the boys awfully hard for long hours in the brutal hot summer. One day a passerby said to the farmer, "You know, you are working those boys awfully hard to raise that much crop; way more effort than what is needed to get the job done." The farmer replied, "That's because I'm not just raising crops. I'm raising boys who will become hard-working young men."

Building Boys

I went to college with Mark Cathy, the grandson of the founder of Chick-fil-A, Truett Cathy, and he was kind enough to send me several of his grandfather's books on life and leadership. One was entitled *It's Better to Build Boys Than Mend Men*. Being a man, I know how difficult it can be, especially having seen my share of broken men, and being broken for many years myself with alcohol issues. We are trained to be tough, which means never being wrong, never backing down, never saying you need help, never saying you are not okay. I see this in women, too, especially single "supermoms" who feel pressure to do everything and make it look effortless and easy while working and maintaining a household. It can be difficult to understand how to raise children who will become hard-working, contributing members of society and who are self-confident and self-reliant enough to take initiative to start new businesses and pursue their dreams.

Truett Cathy believes you shouldn't be in a situation where you have to "mend men." For many of you currently in recovery and on the mend, I applaud your effort in knowing you have the power at any age to still change. Again, as Dr. Joseph said, you can learn self-confidence; it is a skill. And, just like any other skill, like riding a bike or playing the piano, it can be improved by repetition, by doing. The farmer in the story had two objectives—raising crops and raising men, and the metaphor has many parallels. When planting and harvesting crops, you must plant a seed in good soil, you must water and nurture it, wait for it to grow, and then harvest at harvest time. In raising men, there is a value in teaching delayed gratification and the importance of hard work. In some ways, raising men was even more of the farmer's objective, because the impact of what he did would be evident in their lives for many years to come. The farmer pushed them hard because we must be constantly tested and pushed to do better.

Example Story: Two-Mile Time

Dr. Joseph periodically checks the physical fitness of each of his athletes through a test; they must be able to run two miles in under twelve minutes. One to two percent run it in about ten minutes, but about

98 percent run it in just under twelve minutes. Dr. Joseph began to raise the bar and lower the time in increments of thirty seconds every year for the next three years (with the same team: two miles in 11:30, then 11, then 10:30), and monitored each athlete's progress. Every time the same thing happened: 1 to 2 percent of people would be a minute or two ahead of the curve, but the vast majority hovered around the bare minimum time required. Dr. Joseph then translated this same principle to his players' academics at Ryerson.

Minimum GPA

NCAA standards demand that players have a minimum 2.0 GPA to be eligible to play soccer. Dr. Joseph observed his freshmen were "just happy with being good enough," that is, having a GPA that hovered close to 2.0, the bare minimum required. They subsequently later were disappointed in senior year when they wanted to go on to graduate school and realised they had limited options based on their bare minimum GPAS. Dr. Joseph decided to raise the minimum he required above the NCAA standard from 2.0, in small increments, up to 3.0. He noticed each time he raised it, students would begin to hover around the new minimum, thus improving their GPAS by increasing the minimum standard, as he did with the two-mile time. The moral: increase your bare minimum required to increase your overall performance. Many of us tend to do what is required even though we have the capacity to do more. In Dr. Joseph's words, "Have clearly defined goals, not settling with good enough, and if we raise our expectations, [we] will rise to meet them."

Jenn Lim

I was fortunate enough to come across the Delivering Happiness project during my many years of studying the best in class customer service and corporate culture of Zappos. When I was working on my first book, *The Art of Awesome*, I went to visit Zappos' corporate headquarters in Las Vegas after having had a phone interview with their sister project, Delivering Happiness and their Happiness expert Jenn Lim. I found Jenn to be just as powerful and dynamic a leader as Zappo's CEO Tony Hsieh and a delight to talk to.

Jenn Lim's bio says, "From her twenty-plus years of lessons learned in culture and consulting, the proven results from transforming company cultures come back to her simple mission: to inspire science-based happiness, passion, and purpose at work, home, and in everyday life. She has helped over 350 organizations and has devoted her career to cultivate meaningful happiness in companies, communities, and cities around the world."[39] She believes you must "change your world, *then* change the world."

This always resonated profoundly with me. At this writing, we are knee-deep in civil unrest and turmoil. As much as this unrest has a lot to do with the sins of our blood- soaked past, I still believe we do not want to alienate or abdicate personal responsibility and self-governance. To make the world a happier place, we ourselves must first learn to be happy. How do we become happy or increase our level of happiness?

According to the 2019 *World Happiness Report* by the UN, America ranks nineteenth in overall happiness. According to Wikipedia, "The rankings of national happiness are based on a Cantril ladder survey. Nationally representative samples of respondents are asked to think of a ladder, with the best possible life for them being a ten, and the worst possible life being a zero. They are then asked to rate their own current lives on that 0 to 10 scale."[40] Basically, they are asked one simple question, on a scale of 0–10 how happy are you? We would all want to put a 9 or a 10, but many life factors attribute to happiness, and the notion of happiness can be hard to measure or define, as it is subjective.

From what I understand, we have many things that go against us. There are the civil rights issues that have been brought to the forefront, including systemic racism. Then we are confronted with the feeling of having to keep up with the Joneses. But are the Joneses happy, or do they also have that fear of not having or doing or being enough, which

39 "Jenn Lim—Delivering Happiness" https://www.deliveringhappiness.com/jenn-lim.

40 *World Happiness Report*, Wikipedia. https://en.wikipedia.org/wiki/World_Happiness_Report.

is innate in all of us? Is happiness a choice? Can we simply choose to be happy? According to the study of optimism in psychology, we can.

"The Pursuit of Happiness" blog paraphrased the work of Martin Seligman, who they state "is a pioneer of Positive Psychology (the term itself was coined by Abraham Maslow). Seligman found that the most satisfied, upbeat people were those who had discovered and exploited their unique combination of 'signature strengths.'"

Martin summarizes his theory of happiness as using "your signature strengths and virtues in the service of something much larger than you are." Which brings us full circle to the entire premise of this book: that you can be happier if you are more fulfilled, and you can be more fulfilled by tapping into your passion and pursuing your dreams. The reason why so many Americans are so unhappy is because people are taught to believe the lies and myths that there is job security and that you are better off working a job you hate in order to have more stability. While the job might bring you stability (if security even exists), it will certainly not make you happier. If you hate your job and have no outlet for your passion projects, you will be miserable, resentful, and regretful. Many then push it down further with drugs, alcohol, bad relationships, and whatever "gets you through the night," as Frank Sinatra would say, but that by no means is happiness. That is existence.

Jenn Lim tapped into this theory of delivering happiness and extended it by joining the Global Happiness Council of Work and Well-Being since 2017. The GHC identifies best practices at the national and local levels to encourage advancement of the causes of happiness and well-being.[41] It is also a complement to the *World Happiness Reports* and other research on the measurement and explanation of happiness. I really appreciate Jenn taking the time to disseminate all the good works that the Delivering Happiness project is doing and sharing her research and expertise from over twenty years of experience. Lim's unique title of Chief Happiness Officer is something she lives, embodies, and embraces. The pursuit of happiness is a worthwhile ideal we should all

41 "What is the Global Happiness Council?" Global Happiness Council https://www.happinesscouncil.org/council.html.

live, embody, and embrace too. Happiness, if overflowing and in abundance, will spill over into other areas of our lives and eventually out into the world through the work that we do and the people that we help. Happiness is bigger than our bodies, but if we do not cultivate it in our own lives, there is no way we can cultivate it in others. And what does Finland, for three years ranked as the world's happiest country, have that other countries do not? According to news18.com, Finland's Ambassador to India, Nina Vaskunlahti, believes it is because "on a societal level, Finland's success can be attributed to its rigid social safety network, culture of trust, high-quality education, and a strong commitment to gender equality. On a personal level, many Finns cite their connection to nature as an important source of happiness."[42]

So, if you are looking for ways to add more happiness into your own life, start with safety, trust, equality, and connecting to nature! Those are four great pillars to build a foundation of happiness. Now write the prescription for your life and start doing the work you love, not the work you loathe (that is, the work you keep doing based on fear or because of what others want for you). I always tell people the trouble with life is living it. But you will not be able to blame others for your own unhappiness; you ultimately are in control of it. If you want to be happy, you must do something about it. No one else can do it for you, just like no one else can live your life.

Tom Ziglar

I mentioned earlier in the book that one of my all-time favorite interviews was when I went to Ziglar, Inc., headquarters in Plano, Texas, to meet Tom Ziglar, the CEO and son of the legendary author and motivational speaker Zig Ziglar. It was my first interview for *The Art of Awesome* book. I approached him as a budding author, which was easier than approaching him as a musician or anything else. My parents were living

42 Nina Vaskunlahti, "Ambassador of Finland Tells You Why They Are The Happiest," News18, Mar. 2019 https://www.news18.com/news/world/ambassador-of-finland-tells-you-why-they-are-the-happiest-people-in-the-world-2075935.html.

in Plano at the time, so it was a no-brainer for me to reach out to Tom. He was so gracious to give me an autographed copy of the book *Born to Win*, which he co-authored with his late father. I keep the book on my bookshelf as a reminder of how far I have come in my career.

Tom is much more modest and subdued than his father, but still very warm, with a friendly smile and Southern charm, which his father was known for. Tom shared that "the fastest way to success is to replace bad habits with good habits." There is no simpler success formula than that. Our habits are the key to our success—or failure. Are you persevering? Are you dedicated? Are you cultivating the habit to stick with something that is hard, even after the love is gone? Tom did not want to become his father, but he did want to continue his father's legacy. Zig was known for saying, "You can have everything you want if you help enough other people get what they want." What do people want?

People want to be happy. They want to be successful, healthy, and fulfilled. If you start a business providing a service that helps people do any of these things, you will ultimately be successful too. Tom's mission as CEO is to boldly take "Ziglar, Inc., into the world of social communities, Twitter, blogs, and live video webcasts to present the tried-and-true message of hope, integrity, and positive thinking to a whole new audience."

Leave A Legacy

I love both the Ziglars' ideas of leaving a legacy. I learned about Zig through Dave Ramsey, who also taught me a lot about legacy as well. You need to plant seeds for trees you will never sit under. There are many cultures that live each day as if they are dying and work hard to ensure the next generation is taken care of. I recently watched the premiere of the nine episodes of the *Wealth Breakthroughs* series; and episode 8 has a bonus episode with entrepreneur Rick Sapio, who discusses why others are successful and how his dad set him up for success. He explains how his dad knew he was dying in his late forties, and he left his children a document explaining how they should shape their lives once he was gone. It talked about values, key learnings from his life, and all that a kid would need to be able to carry on without a parent.

Sapio told an interesting story about an ex-slave who never wanted his family to go through what he suffered in American slavery. This ex-slave created a legacy document (which was difficult since he was illiterate and had to learn to read and write in his forties) that would help guide future generations. The document centered around marriage and education. His descendants now number about three hundred. None of them has ever divorced, and all obtained a college degree as prescribed in their forefather's legacy document.

What would be in your legacy document? I ask everyone I interview on my *Deeper Grooves* podcast what they want their legacy to be. People always say it is a hard question. I think we don't get out of life what we want the most because we often avoid the hard questions. The idea of legacy should not be a scary subject, even though the idea of death can frighten many. I want to leave a long legacy in all forms of media (music, spoken word, books) that allows me to be as creative as possible, to inspire the next generation, and to show people there is a way you can do it too—at any time and at any level.

Some never try because they are afraid to fail; others are waiting for the perfect situation. Time is ticking. We are going through a worldwide pandemic; as of this writing, 1.71 million people have died—many of them young. I'm sure many did not leave behind a legacy document. Many left behind very little in terms of creating or building wealth. I am not saying everyone should die rich, but even if you had nothing, you could still write down your best ideas and leave them for the next generation to learn from, even if just to learn from your mistakes.

I hope none of you ever must live through the tragedy of a loved one leaving behind nothing but debt, secrets, lies, and problems. I had an ex-girlfriend whose mother passed away. Afterward, the family was a wreck. She had no will and the house she owned went into probate. Her car was left in a parking lot to be towed away to an impound lot, and the tension in the family tore what was left of it apart. It was tough, as the helpless boyfriend, to watch. Death alone is tragic, but the aftermath can be brutal. Is that the legacy of pain, turmoil, and strife you want to leave behind?

Don't think of legacy as having to make a grand gesture. The ex-slave only had two main caveats: stay married (family is important) and go to college (education is important). It goes without saying that if he hadn't been a slave, he would have had more options and opportunities, but I mention his story because I like the simplicity of it. What are the two most important things you would want to tell your loved ones to carry on after your death?

My Legacy Statement

Be you 100 percent, and do whatever you can do with what you are given, to the best of your ability, while always continuing to improve upon those abilities. Pastor T.D. Jakes preaches this message (paraphrased): "You are not responsible for what God did not give you. He gave one man five talents, and one man two talents, and they both doubled what they had 100 percent, and God was pleased. It was the one with one talent who did nothing that God was not pleased with." Don't bury your talent. Even if you have only one, use it to the best of your ability.

Rick Sapio says that if you do not realize how your childhood shaped your worldview and influenced how successful you will be, it will have a tremendous impact on your output. He says that you must do the inner work. I spent so much time in my adult life learning all the things I wish I had known sooner and evaluating everything I had learned and observed from childhood. If something you learned or observed from childhood is not serving you well, you have the power to cast it out, to trample it, to run over it, to put it out of your mind completely, or to do the exact opposite if it leads to a better outcome. Let your legacy be: "I made my own path." Then people can easily follow because you showed them the way.

Still Awesome After All These Years

This message is for anyone who ever had a false start. When I started *The Art of Awesome* book some years back, it took a lot of initiative and faith to step out and tell people that I was a writer even before I had written one solitary word on the page, let alone asked people for an interview. I had no formal training in interviewing, but I had a passion to learn and to speak to people who knew more than I did. I only got about twelve to fifteen pages into a rough draft before I shelved the book idea and never returned to it until now. It does my heart glad to know the ideas from that book can live on in this book, in this chapter, and that even though I had a false start, that misstep eventually led me to this point.

This is not the first or last false start I will have in life. I had the same false start with my first band, and then again with my *Gospel* album. Going back to the drawing board gives you a chance to learn from every failure, every misstep, every misshapen moment, and create something better than what was before. I knew all along that I was awesome and that there was something awesome inside of me that I wanted to get out into the world. I knew there were other awesome people out there who knew more than I do, who were living out their version of awesome every day, and I wanted to study them and learn from them. This is exactly what you should be doing. Life is full of teachers, but unfortunately it is not full of students who are ready to learn. As we've discussed, you can learn in a classroom, but ultimately you learn by doing what it is that you love and doing it despite countless mistakes. If I hadn't had my first band, I would not have my project now. If I hadn't had my first false start for my album, I would never have made my LP. If I hadn't had a false start for my first podcast, I would not have my subsequent podcasts. And if I hadn't had my false start with my first book, I would not have this book now.

The 10,000-Experiment Rule

I don't think anything I have been through is new to the world. No one says the first time you try something you have to knock it out of the park. In fact, most likely you will not. I recently read an *Observer* article stating that people should forget Malcolm Gladwell's 10,000-hour rule (that is, in order to master something you need to do it for 10,000 hours) and adopt the 10,000-experiment rule instead. Michael Simmons, author of the article, explains that Thomas Edison spent a year with a team on thousands of experiments to create the modern-day light bulb. Edison holds a special place in my heart for being the first person to record sound, and I recently discovered he was the founder of GE. Edison can be equated to the titans of the new school, like Jeff Bezos, who also says, "Our success at Amazon is a function of how many experiments we do per year, per month, per week, per day." Walter Isaacson, Da Vinci biographer, states about Leonardo that "every morning his life hack was to make a list of what he wanted to know."[43]

You don't have to be a scientist to adopt a scientific approach to how you experiment with life. What do you want to know? What do you want to do? Who do you want to be? The first time you do something it is usually hard, but then over time it becomes a little easier. For me, the second time is usually much smoother because I have all the things I learned from the first time. After I made my *Gospel* album, which took me two years, it took much less time for other projects because I had found better ways to record—for example, recording most of the band performing together versus recording one at a time.

Every situation calls for something different and will have its own challenges, but when you have been around the block a few times, you start to recognize patterns and foresee problems and solutions. How does one achieve this knowledge? By doing. Do whatever you want, but start right now. You will probably fall flat on your face, but you will get back up and continue to stumble your way through until you get to the other side.

Life has a natural order and natural progression, and you have the benefits of learning from all those who have come before you in the same way that Edison did. Not only did Edison conduct thousands of his own experiments; he undoubtedly learned something from the "twenty-three others [who] had already invented early versions called arc lamps," according to author Michael Simmons. Why would Edison want to learn from these other scientists? Simple: They probably did thousands of experiments too! Which means that Edison had the benefit of 240,000 experiments (twenty-four scientists, including Edison, multiplied by 10,000 experiments) by the time he created his light bulb.

Reading books by Tim Ferris and Tony Robbins, I learned that many of the best in their field try to take this approach and life hack how they can do it faster to achieve ultimate results. Tony Robbins says when he

43 Michael Simmons, "Forget about the 10000 hour rule" http://michaeldsimmons.com/forget-about-the-10000-hour-rule-thomas-edison-jeff-bezos-and-mark-zuckerberg-follow-the-10000-experiment-rule/.

was learning how to become a better salesman or speaker, if the best person in his office was doing ten calls a day, he would do ten calls an hour. If they were giving one speech a month, he would give five a week; thus he would exceed by five or ten times his opponents, getting results in a month that would take the other guys years. You could do this in theory as well—do more experiments a day than your counterparts, eclipse them in a fraction of the time—if you put your mind to failing forward more often.

If Edison had had the mindset every time he failed to give up, then we might still be in the dark. The scientific method allows for failure. Every time you fail you learn something, then you adjust. Einstein said the definition of insanity is doing the same thing over and over and expecting a different result. An experimenter is always trying something new based on the information gained from previous experiments. How often do you go back and review what you have done in the past and find ways to improve upon your future? Technology changes every twelve to eighteen months, and you should be rapidly changing every day.

Read And Apply

CEOS read on average five books a month, according to a study published in *Medium*. And 27 percent of the general population doesn't read at all. If you are one of those people who doesn't read, and you see you are not getting ahead, then reading a book every now and then would help you move the needle forward in your life.

CEOS don't just stop at reading books; they apply that knowledge to whatever they are doing currently to improve. Authors most likely have had ten thousand experiments in their own lives, and the CEO is experimenting daily too. And the subjects of many books have also done their ten thousand experiments. A book can represent millions of experiments all condensed and concentrated.

Never Too Old, Never Too Late

Edison was thirty-six when he decided to tackle the light bulb, and he never thought once that he could not do it, that he was too old, or too late to the game after the other twenty-three people had created similar inventions. He also did not stop at the light bulb but went on to "pioneer five different multibillion-dollar fields: electricity, motion pictures, telecommunications, batteries and sound recording," according to Simmons. He built a factory of inventions.

Will all of us become Edison? Probably not. Just like we may not all become Branson or Jobs or Bezos or Musk or Blakely or Winfrey. But we still must try. We still have to experiment even if twenty-three others have already done something great in our field or even if we are a little late to the game, or a little older, or had false starts, or are not fully prepared to do ten thousand experiments and don't have a team of brilliant minds working alongside us.

When Tony Robbins started, he just had himself and his mind, but he made sure to learn from the best to become the best. That is what I want for myself, and that is what I want for you. I live my entire life to be an example of what can be. I still have a lot of room to grow, but in my circle, I have gotten way more done than many, and many have gotten way more done than me. We can all look back at our body of work and see what we have done. Some people have a lot of debt but nothing tangible to show for it. But many of us can show we've had a lot of time on earth and can easily point to something we have achieved or created. Not everyone has to be all about creation or all about achieving, but odds are, if you are reading this, then you want more out of life and you are trying to figure out how to do it. So, go ahead and embark on "deliberate experimentation," ten thousand experiments, just like Thomas Edison. Maybe that is why the universal symbol for an idea popping into your head is a light bulb?

Answer These Questions:

1. Who are some mentors you can seek out to learn from?
2. What do you need to spend 10,000 experiments doing to become better?
3. How can you incrementally start to increase your personal best?
4. How will you actively pursue your own happiness?

Conclusion

> *"The dream is free. The hustle is sold separately."* —Unknown

It Can Be You And It Can Be Now

When I hear someone give an award acceptance speech in which they say, "I never dreamed this would be possible," I am often reminded of my Sunday school teacher telling me, "That's stinkin' thinkin'." Zig Ziglar taught that you have to "expect to win," which is why I enter contests even if I know I don't have a ghost of a chance of winning. Because you have to be in it to win it. This is exactly what happened to me with the John Lennon Songwriting Contest. I submitted my song "Confident" through the online portal and had already had some success on two Spotify playlists. I noticed that artists I admired, like George Clinton and Flea from the Red Hot Chili Peppers, were judges who would decide who would ultimately win the contest. The day I won, I received an email, which I thought was going to be the general, "Thanks for your entry; here is the list of the people you can hate for the next twelve months," only to learn that I had won a lot of great prizes! What?! Yep. For my song entry, I won over eight thousand dollars in musical goodies from some of the top brands for musical instruments and software. But I could not accept it alone—the song featured Mestizo Beat, who co-wrote the song.

In my wildest dreams, I had never imagined winning that contest or other similar contests for many, many years. As I get older, I have a lingering doubt, thinking, *Should I give up?* But I always somehow find the strength to keep going, and you know why that is? Because I keep saying to myself, "It can be you, and it can be now." Why can't it be you? Don't you deserve good things? Aren't you capable of working hard and making something great that people will appreciate? I believe you are, and I believe you can, but it will only happen if you believe it. If you didn't know this or believe it before, you can start believing it for yourself now. Walk in that newfound knowledge and go create something grand, something wonderful. You owe it to yourself to try.

Passion + Purpose = Fulfillment

If you find yourself running out of steam from unfulfilling work and a bad, self-fulfilling prophecy that you'll never amount to anything of significance, stop right there and take a deep breath. What you are suffering from is not exhaustion. What you are plagued with is living a passionless and purposeless life. And you are not alone. The world is full of people just trying to make it through the day, with no real plan, no focus, no determination, most likely because it has been beaten out of them. Just like the "pursuit of happiness," you must pursue passion and pursue purpose. It does not just fall into your lap. In this book, we have covered numerous ideas about what you can do. Do whatever it takes to figure out your purpose and what you are passionate about and go live that out in work or in play every single day. You'll be happy that you did.

You, Inc. Needs A Makeover

If I were you, I'd fire the old you. The you that is holding you back. The you that is not producing or living up to your full potential. This is what companies do all the time. The reason great companies can do this strategically and easily is because they remain emotionless in business. You are too close to you; thus your emotions get in the way and keep you from doing the inevitable—firing you. If you know deep down inside that I am right, and that you could do better, give yourself x amount of days to improve. Just like you have quarterly and annual reviews with top management at your job, you need to take a weekly, monthly, quarterly, and yearly review of what you are doing with your life, then analyze if you are getting out of it what you want. As mentioned earlier, Socrates said, "The unexamined life is not worth living." Hemlock may have killed Socrates' body, but living a mediocre existence would have killed his soul.

Start Now

As someone who cares about you, I would like to say shut the hell up and get the f$!k up and start doing something. As Bob Marley said, "Open your eyes, and look within; are you satisfied with the life you're living?" If you are not, it's time to "stir it up." Get moving. An object in motion stays in motion, but a sedentary object is in a perpetual state of inertia. You can start at any time. At five or forty-five; it does not matter. Starting is nothing more than a decision to act. I have heard people say that making the decision happens in a split second. The work before or after may take a lifetime, but the initial spark of change can be instantaneous. Remember that you do not have to be great to start, but you must start to be great.

Go Only For The Goal

For all of you with ADHD out there, I feel your pain. For the rest of you who are just unfocused and easily distracted, it happens to the best of us. There is no shortage of digital and physical distractions keeping us from our best work and best life. Zig Ziglar is often quoted as saying, "If you aim at nothing, you will hit it every time." Only a fool aims at nothing and has no goals. Like Luther Vandross, you "don't want to be a fool."

In writing this book I set a page-per-day goal. I rushed to get it done at breakneck speed. At the time of this writing, I am a few days from my end goal date to be done with my first draft. If I had not set an aggressive goal and stuck to it, the likelihood of me completing it would be far less. When I set out to do in a year the P90 fitness program, I set that as a goal with markers to track. When I made my records, I set goals for completion. Not everything worked like clockwork and got done on time, but it all started with a human, an "I can," and a plan.

Thrival Isn't A Word, But It Should Be

You made it to this point, and you have survived. Pat yourself on the back, but don't sit down and rest just yet; the fun isn't over. Survival just means you have a seat at the table, but thriving is contributing to the conversation. Many people have lived, but few are remembered for a long time after their death. I believe a man or woman is measured by what they did with their lives. When we all get to the pearly gates, or judgment day, and we see everything that we have done, there will be good and bad moments. We hope the good outweighs the bad, and we would want our achievements to outweigh our failures. I was recently in a book-writing seminar held by Brian Tracy, who said "Eighty percent of people want to write a book but only 1 percent will follow through." Why do you think that is? Because it is *bleeping* hard, to dedicate fifty to one hundred hours writing 200 to 300 pages. The 79 percent of people who never write or finish the book that has been inside them since forever are surviving. Where do you want to be? In the winner's circle, with cheers and accolades, or on the sideline spectating? Think about what it will take to thrive instead of just survive and focus your sights on doing whatever it takes to get there.

Give Lower-Level Tasks To Someone Else

Nothing makes me happier than pawning off work that I do not want to do to someone else, and I will gladly pay them for it to free up time. When my maid comes to clean, I know that during those two hours I can go exercise, go out to eat, run errands, or see a friend. The maid can come and clean without me being there, but the maid cannot write this book, or record music, or interview someone for my podcast. You need to spend your waking hours working on the projects that fulfill you and propel your life forward. If you can afford to pay someone to get stuff done for you while you are working your day job or your side projects, then you have no reason not to. If money is an issue, offer to barter. I have traded music lessons for studio time, or marketing help, and many people I know have employed interns, and I have had several virtual assistants. If you put your mind to it, you will find a way to make it happen. If it is work that doesn't need to involve you, don't be involved.

Get Your Side Hustle On

It's time to start making some moves. You have more capacity to do more things and get more done—you just have to create a plan and start acting on it. About 90 percent of the work you do will be done using the 10 percent of the time you took to plan. Start planning how you can fit more hours into your day to invest in your side hustle. Even waking up an hour earlier and going to bed an hour later gives you two extra hours a day or fourteen extra hours a week to dedicate to whatever will make you feel more fulfilled if you have self-discipline, stay dedicated, and block out all distractions. Is it easy? No. But is it worth it? Absolutely!

It Can't Be Work All The Time

This is one of the life lessons I struggle with the most. I never take vacation, and I never take days off. I have learned, however, that the body does need to recharge, and the time off may lead you to your "eureka" or "aha" moment. The Ancient Greek scholar Archimedes, when thinking about a complex math problem, discovered the solution when he went to take a bath. You might not become a Rhodes Scholar or candidate for Mensa. But for me, some of my best ideas came from divergent thinking; when I start working on something else unrelated, other ideas appear out of thin air. I am sure this happens to you too. You have worked hard, and when you hit the law of diminishing returns, take a break, take a walk, take a hike, take a joy ride, or take the day off. Your mind and body will thank you. Don't worry, the weekend will end soon enough, and you'll be back to work before you know it.

Learn From The Very Best

Why did we get rid of apprenticeships? No, I am not talking about the show *The Apprentice*, I am talking about real apprenticeships like blacksmiths and cobblers used to have back in the day, when people studied under the tutelage of a master craftsman for several years, usually taking over his craft once deceased or retired. There is something to be said for learning from people who have already done it, who have already learned the tips and tricks. Whether you become a doctor, or banker, or candlestick maker, you would have the advantage of someone else's knowledge and expertise and you could ask them questions, study their process, and pick their brain. Why wouldn't you do that? Internships in this country have been relegated to slave labor, as an errand boy running to get coffee, where apprenticeships provide much more meaningful work. If you could truly apprentice under someone great, you'd be a fool not to.

Call To Action

I hope that the knowledge in this book has helped you move closer to taking swift action toward pursuing your dreams, desires, goals, and aspirations. Don't be like the dog in Les Brown's story who whines and complains about the nail in his side but never moves away from it or does anything about it. How many of you have been like that dog? But you're not a dog, right? You are a human being. I know that each one of you can live richer and fulfilling lives, because I am no different from you. There is nothing special about me; the only difference is I decided to do something and I keep moving the needle forward. If you do decide to do something, and this book has motivated you and inspired you, drop me a line at cliff@sidehustleandflow.net, I would love to hear from you. I wish you well on your journey of self-discovery and fulfillment. I will see you in the winner's circle. Thank you for reading. I hope you enjoyed perusing it as much as I have enjoyed writing it. I have no doubt that if you apply 10 percent of what you have read here, you will be ten times closer to success. Cheers to your success!

You can be more fulfilled by finding and living out your purpose if you change your mindset and add practicality and intentionality to each day.

About the Author

Soul music artist Cliff Beach has been performing live for more than 18 years in Los Angeles. The Berklee-trained singer/songwriter/keyboardist and DC native has created a style of music he coins as "Nu-funk", a hybrid of soul, traditional R&B, funk, and neo-soul which he performs regularly throughout Southern California. In 2013, Cliff released the highly anticipated "Who the Funk is Cliff Beach?" EP, independently, which was nominated for three LA Music Awards including "Record of the Year" and one Hollywood Music in Media award. Cliff also received national press in a featured live review in *Music Connection Magazine* in Nov. 2013 and was a featured performer at TEDX Napa Valley in March 2014. Cliff's last album entitled "The Gospel According to Cliff Beach", which was nominated for an Independent Music Award (Funk/Fusion Jam Album); winner of 2 Global Music Awards. Cliff is a voting Member of NARAS, a Songwriter and Publisher with BMI, and his single "Confident" is featured on Spotify All Funked Up and Funk Drive playlists with over 500k+ streams, winner of 2 Global Music Awards and the John Lennon Songwriting Contest Grand Prize in R&B, and also recently featured in a BMW Motorrad USA commercial. He is also the host of the Deeper Grooves Podcast and Deeper Grooves Radio Hour on 885FM KCSN.